BARTÓK his life and times

BARTÓK
his life and times

Hamish Milne

MIDAS BOOKS
Tunbridge Wells

HIPPOCRENE BOOKS
New York

In the same illustrated documentary series

General Editor: William Eden, MA (Cantab)

Designed by David Morley-Clarke

© Hamish Milne 1982

First published UK in 1982 by
MIDAS BOOKS
12 Dene Way, Speldhurst,
Tunbridge Wells, Kent TN3 0NX.

ISBN 0 85936 273 6 (UK)

First published USA in 1982 by
HIPPOCRENE BOOKS INC
171 Madison Avenue,
New York. NY 10016.

ISBN 0 88254 659 7 (US)

Printed and bound in Great Britain by
The Pitman Press, Bath

Contents

Bartók on an early folk song
collecting tour.

Chapter One

Without a comprehensive knowledge of the political and geographical upheavals which attended the prolonged death-throes of the Austro-Hungarian Empire, it can be a baffling task to track down the birth-place of one of Hungary's greatest sons. One might assume, rightly, that Béla Bartók was born in Hungary, but even the knowledge that he was born on 25th March, 1881 in Nagyszentmiklós, Torontál county, is of limited help, since no such place is to be found on any modern map of the country. If one recalls that a large part of eastern Hungary was ceded to Romania in the peace treaties of 1920, then you still need to know that Nagyszentmiklós was then renamed Sînnicolaul Mare. It is as well to get to grips with the geographical vagaries and polyglot population of the region, as they have an important, indeed crucial bearing on the life and work of the composer, who, it should be remembered, was for long widely referred to as 'pianist, composer and folk-song collector'. Bartók's nationalism will be seen to have sprung from a fiercely racial pride, rather than the sentimental attachment to scenic characteristics, domestic or political traditions, or even the 'homeland' which plays such a central rôle in the nationalist fervour of many more romantic patriots.

Indeed, racial and linguistic tension, that most intractable of all political problems, lay at the heart of the unrest and upheavals that eventually led to the disintegration of the Hapsburg empire and to the formation of the states which make up eastern Europe today. With the benefit of hindsight, it is not difficult to perceive that the Hapsburg monarchy had been fighting a losing battle since the French revolution. Its political achievement in the hundred and twenty years or so which intervened between then and its eventual dissolution can be measured only in its success in delaying defeat. The more or less bloody suppression of revolutionary movements in Austria, Hungary, Czechoslovakia, Poland and Italy (to give them their modern names) in the mid-nineteenth century was effective in restoring an illusion of stability, but, as always, such measures inflamed rather than dampened the underlying aspirations which motivated them. The defeat of Lajos Kossuth's Hungarian insurgents in 1849 was, in the words of Zoltán Kodály, still a grim and living memory. Old men who had taken part in the uprising and who still wore their beards in the style of Kossuth, were still to be seen frequently in the streets.

Red-blooded patriots were unappeased by the Compromise of 1867 (the *Ausgleich*), hastily put together by Austria in the wake of reverses suffered in Italy, which established the so-called Dual Monarchy and introduced a loose package of conservative and liberal measures which more or less negated one another, so unrest continued to simmer beneath the surface.

In Hungary, the revolutionary undercurrents were two-fold, and the various movements were only united in their allegiance to an undefined concept of a 'Hungarian Hungary'. Although it is not always apparent to the protagonists, separatist and proletarian movements are not synonymous and their aims can readily come into conflict, even opposition. In nineteenth century Hungary the repression of the common man stemmed at once from foreign domination and from the power of an unusually numerous and largely feudal-minded aristocracy.

Bartók's nationalism bridged both camps and when, early in his career, it became central to his artistic manifesto, it gave rise to

Below Bartók's father who died when the composer was seven years old.
(Embassy of the Hungarian People's Republic)

Right Bartók's mother who initiated his musical training.

Nagyszentmiklósi m. kir. földmives iskola főépülete (igazgatói lak.)

Örvendtünk a sikerült aro képnek, köszönet érte. Sok a dolgom, levélben legközelebb többet. csókol: A.

903. VII/18

The Agricultural School at Nagyszentmiklós where Bartók's father was headmaster.

bitter dissentions amongst officials and intellectuals over the validity of his extra-musical objectives. The petty squabbles which followed Hungarian performances of his music and the planning and publication of his researches into folk-music had little to do with their intrinsic artistic or scholastic value.

However, it seems unlikely that Bartók's immediate family was much affected by political discontent for in the two preceding generations they had made for themselves a modest but secure niche in the established order of things. Later, in his student years, Bartók was to chide his mother (and none too lightly) for her unpatriotic lapses into German in the family circle. His grandfather, János, had secured the respectable post of headmaster of the agricultural school of Nagyszentmiklós, and on his death in 1877, the composer's father, Béla senior, succeeded him at the early age of twenty-two. Three years later he married Paula Voit, an accomplished amateur pianist and teacher and in the following year their first child, Béla, was born.

To record the secure middle-class situation of the family should not imply any complacency or lack of imagination in the young parents. On the contrary, Bartók's father seems to have been an unusually energetic and imaginative man, his sense of civic duty enlivened by his enterprise and determination. He drew up extensive plans for farming reform and intensification, as well as writing quite copiously on educational matters. Of more

9

Bartók and his sister in Poszony, 1892.

significance in the present context are his cultural interests which were wide but particularly favoured music. He was a leading light in the establishment of the Nagyszentmiklós Music Society, and even learnt the 'cello so that he could play in its orchestra. Although predominantly Hungarian, the town had large and vociferous German, Romanian and Yugoslav communities, and to reconcile the different groups was in itself no mean feat.

The musical initiation and development of the infant Béla was largely in the affectionate hands of Paula Bartók, and it is lovingly recorded in her account of the composer's childhood. It reveals little more than one would expect from an exceptionally musical child, a ready ability to play folk tunes on the piano with one finger and so forth, hardly intimations of genius. Like any good middle-class family, the Bartóks nurtured the child's talent by playing to him and taking him to local performances, such as the inaugural concert of the Music Society orchestra. Of this occasion, Paula Bartók recalled, with a trace of doting motherliness,

The other guests went on eating and drinking but he put down his knife and fork at once and listened with complete absorption. He was delighted, but annoyed that the other people could go on eating while such beautiful music was being played.

At the age of five, at his own insistent request, he began to receive piano lessons from his mother, and all seemed set for a comfortable bourgeois childhood. But a cruel event was to make the coming years a period of bitter hardship and struggle. Bartók's father had suffered continuing ill-health and, despite holidays and 'cures' in Austria, he was forced to give up his job at the end of 1887. However, his deterioration was unabated and he died on August 4th of the following year.

So poor Paula Bartók found herself bereft of her husband, with no means of support and two children to care for (a daughter, Elza, was now three years old). Her elder sister, Irma, came to live in the house and helped as best she could, while Paula continued for the time being to give piano lessons. Béla had already shown a tendency towards introversion from an early age, and was often ill. Severe chest infections were frequent and his reluctance to play or communicate with other children was aggravated by an unsightly skin complaint. The present crisis and his mother's inevitable preoccupation with practical considerations can only have made his feeling of isolation worse. Throughout his life he left an impression of extreme reserve on all who met him, though few doubted the iron will and unbending principles which lay behind his withdrawn demeanour, and to which he was not afraid to give voice in the face of powerful opposition, as we shall see.

10

After a year or so, as is the nature of these things, the family began to emerge from the shadow of their tragedy and look more positively to the future. Paula found a job teaching at a school in Nagyszöllös, now in Czechoslavakia. They stayed there for three years, during which time Béla's musical development regained its momentum. He began composing short pieces for piano and his talent began to attract the attention of local and visiting musicians. Mrs Bartók was sensibly resistant to predictions of a 'great future' for her boy and sent him off to school in Nagyvárad where her other sister Emma could look after him. It was not a great success, and he returned the following year to Nagyszöllös, but his musical achievements were greater than his academic ones and he appeared with great success at a local concert, playing the difficult first movement of Beethoven's *Waldstein* sonata and his own composition *The Flow of the Danube*. It would be foolish to pretend to foresee greatness in this naïve little tone-poem, but it shows the creative urge emerging, albeit uncertainly. More important, this modest local triumph sufficiently impressed a school inspector who was instrumental in securing for Paula a year's leave of absence. She wasted no time in removing the family to the infinitely more glamorous Pozsony (now Bratislava), an important cultural centre, where she hoped to find a better job for herself and better education for her children. It was not a happy venture, as the job did not materialise and, at the end of her leave, she was forced to accept a post in Beszterce which was considered even less exciting than Nagyszöllös. Her persistence was finally rewarded, though, when,

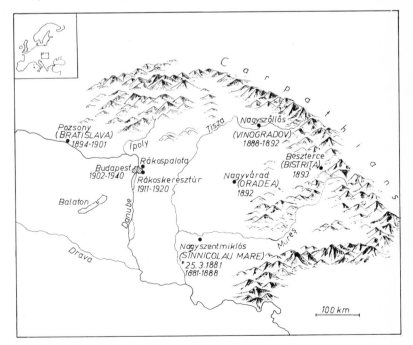

Biographical map of Bartók's early years.

11

in 1894, she was accepted onto the staff of the Teacher Training College in Pozsony. So the five year period of rootless wandering was over.

For Béla, the change was of inestimable benefit.

'In those days,' he wrote in a brief autobiography (published in 1923), 'Pozsony had the most flourishing musical life of all Hungarian provincial towns.'

On the previous, abortive attempt to settle in Pozsony, he had started lessons with László Erkel, the third of four sons (all musicians) of Ferenc Erkel, a composer revered in Hungary, whose operas are still regularly performed at the Budapest Opera. These lessons were now eagerly resumed:

He taught me harmony and the piano until my fifteenth year, and made me go to the opera and to concerts . . . Nor did I neglect to take part in chamber music, so by my eighteenth year I had a pretty good knowledge of music from Bach to Wagner (though only up to *Tannhäuser*). In between, I got down to composition; I was strongly influenced by Brahms and Dohnányi who was four years my senior and whose early work made a deep impression on me.

László Erkel, son of Ferenc Erkel, who taught Bartók in the early 1890s.

Dohnányi was an important figure in Hungarian music, and becoming well-known throughout Europe. An outstanding pianist and teacher and fine conductor, he composed warmly appealing music of immense technical accomplishment in an unashamedly post-Brahmsian style. His elaborate *Variations on a Nursery Song* ('Twinkle Twinkle Little Star' to English speakers) for piano and orchestra remains one of the best of all musical jokes and a witty and invigorating piece in its own right. For a time it seemed as though Bartók was going to be yet another composer in the same mould, and it has to be said that, on the evidence of his earliest works, he was not as good at it as Dohnányi. Of course, when he found his true identity and blossomed into one of the great original voices of twentieth century music, the styles of the two diverged irreconcilably. It is to Dohnányi's credit, though, that his own conservatism did not prevent him from retaining a keen interest in the apparent barbarisms and asperities of the younger man.

In all, then, these five years in Pozsony were a time of retrenchment, of consolidation. The traumas of his father's death and lack of a settled home were laid to rest, and Béla made steady progress towards musical maturity. He put in those long hours of piano practise without which no pianist can contemplate a serious career as a performer, and his knowledge and understanding of the accumulated legacy of the great masters increased daily through his own studies and by the natural absorption of a stimulating musical environment. When László Erkel died in 1896, his work continued

Poszony where Bartók began systematic studies.

without serious hiatus under the now forgotten composer Hyrtl, and as his schooldays drew to an end it was not questioned that his life lay in music.

The geographical, historical and social proximity of Pozsony to Vienna was such that it had longstanding links with the Hapsburg capital, so the choice of conservatoire for Béla to pursue his serious musical studies scarcely merited discussion. In great excitement he set out for Vienna with his mother on December 8th, 1898. He passed his entrance exam with flying colours and was promised a scholarship from the Emperor's private funds, although, with the peculiar inconsistency of autocratic régimes, free places were generally reserved for Austrian-born candidates.

The long suffering Paula was understandably thrilled and bursting with pride. But within a few weeks, Bartók had rejected the offer and made the momentous and far-reaching decision to go instead to the Academy of Music in Budapest. It must have caused a great commotion in the family circle but, characteristically, the autobiography is unemotional and laconic,

At Pozsony in those days the Vienna Conservatoire was considered the only main musical centre. Nevertheless, I followed Dohnányi's advice and chose Budapest.

13

Chapter Two

Musically, as otherwise, Hungary had been very much a satellite of the Austrian empire and in the upper echelons of the aristocracy (who in many cases owed their wealth and influence to their shameless allegiance to the Hapsburg court) there were households who employed sizeable bands of musicians. As a rule, these were imported from Germany or Austria and did much to establish the essentially German-Austrian tradition which dominated Hungarian musical life right up to the early years of this century. Most notable amongst them was Josef Haydn, who was for many years resident composer and musical director to Prince Miklós (Nicholas) Esterházy, so many of the greatest masterpieces of the classical era were in fact composed and first performed in Hungary. Nor was Haydn remiss in acknowledging his debt, as many of his works make reference to the perennial popularity of 'gypsy' fiddling in Hungary. The finale of his G major piano trio, the so-called 'Gypsy Rondo', is but the most celebrated example among many. Zoltán Kodály pointed out that, in so doing, Haydn

was the first to announce to the world at large, in his music inscribed *all'ongarese*, that a musical mode of expression specially Hungarian and differing from any other had come into being.

How far the elements used by Haydn were truly representative of the Hungarian ethos is another matter, and one which was to exercise Bartók and Kodály greatly in their efforts to establish a truly national style. What is beyond argument is the much needed shot in the arm which Haydn, by his very presence, injected into Hungarian musical consciousness. Kodály acknowledged this,

In small Hungarian country towns, wherever there were schoolboys, civil servants or others who could play the fiddle, they sat down and played the string quartets of Haydn. For these people, more often than not, this was the only road leading towards the higher sphere of classical music.

Opposite Bartók in 1899, the year he entered the Budapest Academy.
(Embassy of the Hungarian People's Republic)

The material used by Haydn (and by Schubert and Brahms after him) to add a dash of Hungarian local colour to certain

Budapest around 1903.

compositions derived from two principal sources — the so-called *verbunkos*[1] style, an amalgam of ancient dance music and popular song, and the gypsy *csárdás* of later date. Amidst the political discontent of the nineteenth century this style assumed symbolic status, and Hungarian composers adopted it whole-heartedly as evidence of their patriotic fervour, regardless of its ethnic impurity. Even so, it was largely a cosmetic veneer and composers like Mihály Mosonyi, Ferenc Erkel and the cosmopolitan Liszt remained essentially in the mainstream of Western European romantic music, their devotion to the cause of nationalism notwithstanding. Ferenc Liszt was by far the most celebrated Hungarian musician of his time (his father had been employed on the Esterházy estates) and although he left his native country at an early age he paid increasing attention to Hungarian affairs in later years. This is reflected in his music, where the dashing Hungarian Rhapsodies of his youth give way to the stark 'Hungarian Historical Portraits' and church music in 'Hungarian' style. His visits to Budapest became longer and more frequent and as, in the face of military and political frustration, cultural ideals seemed a positive step towards national identity, he took pride in accepting the position of first president of

1. The word derives from the German *Werbung* (enlisting). Such music traditionally accompanied the recruitment of soldiers.

16

the National Academy of Music, founded in 1875 and Erkel became the first director.

Nationalist aspiration remained buoyant, but musical influences obstinately Germanic. The situation was much the same when Bartók enrolled for his first term at the Academy in September, 1899. Erkel's successor as director was Ödön Mihalovich, an ardent Wagnerian. The Budapest Opera had reached almost international status, but largely through the invigorating musical direction of the great Austrian composer and conductor, Gustav Mahler in the years 1888-91.

Budapest was not untouched by other great forces of the 19th century, capitalism and industrialisation, with their attendant shrinking of the natural barriers of communication. Whereas Pozsony, for the reasons already mentioned, had preserved its close links with Vienna together with a certain bourgeois conservatism, Budapest had succumbed to more glamorous and cosmopolitan influences and was now, if not exactly a playground, certainly as close to Paris in its daily life-style as to Vienna. The casinos, the opulent restaurants were patronised by the still wealthy aristocracy, but the latest literary and political controversies raged in the street cafés. Not that this was likely to distract the intensely serious young Bartók — who was in any case uneasy in company — but he responded to the excitement and variety of the city's cultural life.

His piano professor at the Academy was István Thomán, a former pupil of Liszt and the teacher of Dohnányi, who was to exert a wholly stimulating and benevolent influence. Thomán saw his rôle as an embracing one; his supervision of his pupil's technical and academic progress was allied to a generously humane concern for his general welfare and the growth of his artistic experience. In a tribute to his teacher, written some twenty-five years later, Bartók shows a warmth and affection which he rarely exhibited in public,

A few months after my performance examination — I didn't even think that Thomán would remember me — I received an unexpected letter from him. It was a brief invitation to come to Budapest as his guest to hear the great conductor János (Hans) Richter and the Philharmonic Orchestra play Beethoven's Ninth Symphony, a musical event that he, Thomán, found very important for the development of a young musician. Needless to say, this letter was but the 'upbeat' of his unparalleled, truly paternal concern for me that he demonstrated a countless number of times when I became one of his pupils the next year.

Bartók also had some interesting observations to make on Thomán's teaching methods,

I must have been a real 'savage' as a pianist when I first came to Thomán. My technique was good enough, but thoroughly crude. Thomán taught

Haydn. Portrait in oils by Thomas Hardy.

me the correct position of the hands and all the different 'natural' and 'summarising' movements which the newest pedagogy has since made into a truly theoretical system and which, however, Liszt had already applied instinctively and Thomán, a former pupil of Liszt, could acquire directly from his great master. Thus, the most initiated hands imparted to me the mastery of poetically colouring the piano tone.

Thomán's personal qualities he summarises as a

harmonious entity made up of great circumspection, superior tact, deep love of mankind and superb expertise.

One of the first steps which Thomán took in the interest of his new pupil was to recommend him to János Koessler for composition lessons. The benefits of this encounter are less easy to assess. Koessler was unarguably an immensely capable musician and pedagogue, but a representative of the old school, a staunch Brahmsian and a stickler for correct academic procedures with a mistrust of novelty in any shape or form.

It was particularly unfortunate that this same Brahmsian thinking was precisely what Bartók was struggling to emerge from, having passed through that stage during his year in Pozsony. His bewilderment and depression come through clearly in his letters to his mother almost from the beginning of his lessons with Koessler. In January, 1900,

I took along the quintet. Professor Koessler said that none of it was any good at all, that I should try my hand at simpler things, like songs for example. I have no idea what was so bad about it as he spoke only in general terms — that I should take more care over the choice of themes, and so on. . . . I feel myself that my works are basically sound, but need

István Thomán's piano class of 1901. Bartók stands 3rd from the left. On the extreme left is Arnold Székely, distinguished pianist and teacher of Sir Georg Solti and Annie Fischer. Felicitas Fábian, seated third from the right, was an early flame of Bartók and dedicatee of some early compositions.

modification, mostly in connection with form. But if they are so bad that they can't be improved well, that's pretty serious.

In any event, the result was that Bartók's creative urge all but dried up for a period of about two years. As a composer, he was clearly going through a state of self-examination and reappraisal, and it may be unjust to lay the blame entirely on Koessler. Not that his time was wasted; far from it. He worked enthusiastically and profitably for Thomán and gained ever-increasing respect as a pianist. Although shortage of money was a constant problem, he still managed to take full advantage of the riches of Budapest's musical life. He threw himself wholeheartedly into the study of Wagner's mature works as well as the orchestral music of Liszt, perhaps as a way of exorcising the Brahmsian spirit, and he seldom missed a performance by a great visiting soloist or ensemble. His

19

letters home contain careful evaluations and comparisons of such artists as Eugene D'Albert, Emil Sauer, Jan Kubelik and many more. He had to eke out his allowance by giving piano lessons to achieve all this, and Thomán was helpful here, as always,

he secured me free admission to the Sauer recital and so I was able to sell the ticket I had already bought. And now he's given me a ticket for *The Valkyrie.*

Bartók's health had given his family cause for concern again from the very start of his studentship. In October, 1899, he had gone down with a particularly severe attack of bronchitis and had been forced to return home to recuperate. His doctor was so concerned that he strongly advised that he abandon the stresses and strains of a career in music for something less demanding. This turned out to be an unduly alarmist view. On this occasion the interruption was not too prolonged and he concluded the academic year without any further relapse. However, at the end of the summer vacation, when on the point of returning to Budapest to commence his second year, he was taken ill again. This time it was more serious, a combination of pleurisy and pneumonia. Fears that his life was in danger were perhaps exaggerated, but it was several months before he was fit enough to resume his studies. By then it was too late to join the second year course at the Academy, but he made full use of his time in consolidating his piano technique and learning new repertoire,

Liszt, regarded as the father figure of Hungarian music.

including the monumental *Sonata in B minor* of Liszt, whose powerful personality was insinuating itself more and more into his own musical consciousness. 'The Problem of Liszt' (the title of a paper which Bartók delivered to the Hungarian Academy of Sciences in 1936) was to occupy his thoughts for many a year. Like so many musicians he was puzzled by the paradoxes of the man, the genius tinged with theatricality, sensuality with asceticism. Despite reservations about the work, which he later ascribed to misunderstanding ('of course, at this time, I didn't understand Beethoven's last sonatas either,' he added), he scored a tremendous success when he performed it at an Academy concert in October, 1901.

Despite this and other notable advances as a pianist, the impasse which he had reached in his work with Koessler remained unresolved, although he continued dutifully to produce compositions which were little more than academic exercises done to order.

In his autobiography he recalled the circumstances with detachment, without reference to the agonies of self-doubt he must have suffered,

I got rid of the Brahmsian style, but did not succeed, via Wagner and

Summer in Poszony, 1901.
(Left to right) Bartók (recently recovered from a severe illness), sister Elza, Aunt Irma and Paula Bartók.

Liszt, in finding the new way, so ardently desired. (I did not at that time grasp Liszt's true significance for the development of modern music and only saw the technical brilliance of his compositions). I did no independent work for two years.

However, in the course of his regular attendance at the Philharmonic concerts, 'the new way' opened up before him though not, as it turned out, the road to his true destiny. This time his description of the event leaves us in no doubt of the pent-up frustration from which it brought release,

From this stagnation I was roused as by a lightning stroke by the first performance in Budapest of *Also sprach Zarathustra*. The work was received with real abhorrence in musical circles here, but it filled me with the greatest enthusiasm.

He immediately plunged into a wholesale exploration of Richard Strauss, whose methods, he became convinced, 'held the seeds of a new life.' It was a comparatively short-lived enthusiasm, one might almost describe it as youthful infatuation. With the knowledge we now have of Bartók's later style and creed, Strauss would seem an unlikely hero indeed, an arch-perpetrator of the 'excesses of the Romanticists' from which he turned so decisively but a few years later. But, for now, Richard Strauss was the man of the moment and under his spell Bartók recovered his voice and produced a steady stream of new works. His new obsession also led him to make a piano transcription of Strauss's vast and complex tone-poem *Ein Heldenleben*, of which his brilliant performance gave added lustre to his reputation as a pianist. He was engaged to appear at the prestigious *Tonkünstlerverein* in Vienna specifically on the strength of it. He took a mischievous delight in parading this particular

21

success in front of Koessler who, predictably, had no time for Strauss's post-Wagnerian extravagances.

An agreeable side-effect of this psychological breakthrough (no doubt bolstered by the confidence engendered by his growing status) was a relaxation of his social inhibitions. He began to be seen (and heard) at the various private musical gatherings that were a lively element in the musical and academic life of the city. To Bartók, the most congenial of these meetings were at the house of Emma Gruber who, at this time, was married to a wealthy businessman and amateur violinist. It was here that he first met Zoltán Kodaly, a true kindred spirit, who was to be a life-long confidant and collaborator in all musical matters, especially folk music research and educational projects. This remarkable lady was no mean musician herself, a pianist and composer of genuine attainment, so whether her short course of lessons from Bartók was an exercise in self-improvement or patronage is open to question. In any event, the durability of their friendship was assured when, following a divorce, she married Kodály in 1910.

At the Grubers, too, Bartók renewed his acquaintance with Dohnányi, now renowned as a virtuoso throughout Europe, and arranged to take intensive coaching from him in Gmunden at the end of his final year at the Academy. This had to be arranged clandestinely as Dohnányi, seldom fully master of his own affairs, had too often claimed pressure of work as an excuse to fob off the legions of young pianists who clamoured to study with him.

The richest fruits of this period of regeneration were a group of large-scale compositions which make up the greater part of what is loosely known today as the posthumous works, i.e. those which can be considered an important part of Bartók's *oeuvre* written before the allocation of opus numbers, after discounting juvenilia. A three movement *Sonata for violin and piano* has not found much acceptance, and little is heard of the ambitious and difficult *Four Piano Pieces*. The lavish *Piano Quintet*, published only in 1970, has much to commend it, despite its sometimes clumsy joinery, and it may yet establish itself in the repertoire of a medium that finds favour with audiences though surviving on a handful of masterpieces. But the outstanding achievement of this group is, appropriately, the most luxuriantly Straussian, the so-called *Kossuth Symphony* (more properly *Kossuth — Symphonic Poem for Full Orchestra*), and here, once again, we must digress briefly into the shifting sands of Hungarian politics.

As we have seen, anti-Hapsburg resentment never lay far beneath the surface of everyday life and in 1902-3 a series of events occurred which, at the same time, incited the more spirited elements in the populace to fury and fanned Bartók's own hitherto quiescent political awareness into a raging fire. A bill was put before the

22

Budapest at the turn of the
century.
(Corvina)

Hungarian Parliament proposing an increase in its contribution to
the Imperial army. The Hungarian army with its primary
allegiance to Vienna was a perennial thorn in the flesh of the
separatists, and a symbolic issue was made of the continuing use of
German as the official military language. In fact, German was still
the common language of the upper and middle classes (much as
French was spoken in Russia as a sign of education and sophistica-
tion) and it also served as a means of communication between the
various ethnic groups. But when Emperor Franz Joseph, with
autocratic disdain, bluntly refused to countenance the use of the
Hungarian language in the army, it was denounced as the blackest
treachery, final proof (if such were needed) of the hypocritical sham
of the Compromise of 1867. Civil disturbances were almost daily
events and Bartók passionately added his voice to the general
clamour for freedom from the foreign yoke. He took to wearing
Hungarian national costume to the Academy, berated his mother
and aunt for speaking German and inscribed his letter headings
with nationalist slogans. On a deeper level, far removed from mob
hysteria, he wrote to his mother,

Everyone, on reaching maturity, has to set himself a goal and must direct
all his work and actions towards this. For my own part, all my life, in every

23

sphere, always and in every way, I shall have one objective: the good of Hungary and the Hungarian nation.

What more natural then, as he embarked on his first great orchestral work, his own *Heldenleben*, that his hero should be Lajos Kossuth, defeated leader of the last great Hungarian uprising?

The omens for *Kossuth* were good from the outset. Even Koessler expressed guarded approval at the piano-score and suggested Bartók orchestrate it in the hope of its being included in an Academy concert. But more exciting things were in store. The Budapest Philharmonic decided to present it in January, 1904, and, even better, at a fortuitous meeting in Pozsony during the summer, the great conductor Hans Richter was so impressed that he promised to arrange a performance with the Hallé orchestra in Manchester.

The nationalist scenario was always likely to produce stock responses in Budapest, and the première induced more patriotic slogans than informed comment from the press. In a sense, Bartók had invited this by writing his own rather naïve and provocative programme notes. Each of the ten movements was given an explanatory heading — 'Danger threatens the Fatherland', 'Come fine Hungarian warriors, valiant heroes' and so on. The representation of the Austrian army by a grotesque parody of *Gott Erhalte* (the Austrian national anthem) was too much for some of the non-Hungarian members of the orchestra who downed their instruments in protest at the first rehearsal. This touch of notoriety did no harm at all to the growing reputation of the young composer.

The performance in Manchester aroused no such passions, of course, and Bartók scored a greater success with piano solos by Liszt and Volkmann (which he played in the same programme) than with the symphony. The unbiased listener probably shared the impression we receive today on the rare occasions it is performed; that the work, despite undeniably striking passages, is so closely modelled on Strauss's tone poems that it can only suffer by the inevitable comparisons.

Amidst this welter of activity, Bartók's student days came to an unspectacular, almost incidental conclusion. He was under no delusions. Although he could justifiably feel that he had made an indelible imprint as a composer, it was by playing and teaching that he would have to earn his living in the foreseeable future.

Chapter Three

Bartók's career as a concert pianist had got away to a highly promising start. Even while engaged in the preparation of *Kossuth* he had to break off from time to time to fulfil performing engagements. Moreover, his name was becoming known beyond the Austro-Hungarian border, partly on account of Dohnányi's enthusiastic recommendation. The Liszt scholarship awarded on his graduation from the Budapest Academy enabled him to spend a few months in Berlin where his reputation already was sufficient to attract the presence of at least two great pianists, Busoni and Godowsky, to his recital, and his performance in Manchester had secured him the promise of appearances in London the following year. Nonetheless, there was never any question that he would be diverted by his successes into the comparatively narrow outlook of the travelling virtuoso, and he felt keenly the need for seclusion, not only to pursue his composing but to ponder the philosophical and moral attitudes that gave his life purpose. Accordingly, he retired to the plains of Gerlicepuszta in the spring of 1904 and stayed there for six months, emerging only briefly in August to make the pilgrimage (obligatory for all Wagnerites) to the Bayreuth Festival. There he met again Hans Richter who was greatly taken with Bartók's latest work, a Scherzo for piano and orchestra, another Straussian monster, virtually a fully fledged concerto. But the most interesting product of that summer was the *Rhapsody No. 1* which exists in several versions of which the one for piano and orchestra is definitive. It is not surprising to learn that Bartók was working hard at the preparation of several major pieces by Liszt at the same time as composing this most overtly Lisztian of all his works. He was evidently well pleased with it as it was on this work, along with the Piano Quintet, that he elected to be judged in the Rubinstein competition, held in Paris in the summer of 1905, for which he had entered as both composer and pianist. This expedition to Paris proved to be a harsh experience, but its effect on his outlook and character was perhaps not wholly negative.

From Bartók's point of view the competition was a humiliating fiasco. The piano section was won by the great German pianist Wilhelm Backhaus whom Bartók conceded to be an entirely worthy opponent, without accepting that he was necessarily a better player in any absolute sense.

'It's a matter of taste whose performance you prefer,' he declared.

It was in the composers' competition, however, that he tasted the real bitterness of failure. The facts presented to the public were simply that the jury had decided not to award either of the cash prizes, but to confer Certificates of Merit on two competitors, the Italian Attilio Brugnoli and Bartók, in that order. What roused Bartók's disappointment into a fury of frustration was, firstly, the incompetent organisation of the practical arrangements for the competition and, secondly, some inside information given him by Lajos Dietl (an old friend, then teaching in Vienna) who was on the panel of judges.

On arrival, Bartók was told that there were mistakes in the orchestral parts of the *Rhapsody*, which he quickly corrected, only to be told that it was too difficult for the orchestra to rehearse in the time available. However, the officials had not reckoned with the tenacity of the young composer and in the face of his stubborn insistence they gave way and 'it was finally played rather well, after all.'

He was not so successful with the *Quintet* and was told 'flatly and categorically' that it could not be learned in time — this after they had insisted that he copy out a second score for the jury to follow during the performance. He was therefore forced to substitute his Violin Sonata (which luckily he had with him) and after an anxious search was fortunate enough to secure a fine violinist, the young Russian Lev Zeitlin, to play it with him.

No wonder, then, that Bartók's letter to his mother fairly fumes with rage at the eventual outcome,

The minute I receive my diploma of (dis)honour, I shall send it back to Auer,[1] to Petrograd. I am not prepared to accept rubbish like that.

I may say that Brugnoli's pieces are absolutely worthless conglomerations. It is quite scandalous that the jury could not see how much better my works are.

And yet my works were quite well performed. That, having heard them, the jury still failed to appreciate them is equally scandalous.

On the face of it, this seems nothing but a petulant outburst of wounded vanity, but Bartók was particularly upset by Lajos Dietl's disclosure that the preponderance of Russian judges, 'where they play nothing but Haydn, Mozart and Beethoven' (not strictly true), gave little or no chance to works in a more advanced idiom. Accord-

---

1. Leopold Auer (1845-1930) chairman of the jury. Hungarian-born violinist who founded a celebrated violin school in Russia. Jascha Heifetz was among his many famous pupils.

ing to Dietl, Richard von Perger, a Viennese Brahmsian, simply couldn't understand it at all, to which Auer added airily, 'Oh yes, this is the new school; we're already too old for anything like that.'

Nor was this the most acandalous of Dietl's revelations. The Russian composer and pianist Anton Rubinstein had bequeathed a capital sum to the Petrograd Conservatoire on which interest amounting to 10,000 francs was to accrue every five years to fund the prizes for the competition. Russian currency had been devalued in the wake of the war with Japan and there was a suggestion that, as a result, the interest fell short of the advertised prize money, the inference being that there had been a tacit agreement all along to withhold prizes to avoid drawing on the capital.

'If that is so,' wrote Bartók venomously, 'it was a monstrous piece of impudence and deception to allow all the composer competitors to flock to the place on a wild-goose chase.'

This blow to his confidence had deep-rooted effects which lingered for several years, but at the same time accelerated his quest for a definitive personal style which, despite his pride in his recent works, he realised had not yet crystallised.

For the time being, he was not so despondent as to be blind to the marvels of Paris — 'this heavenly godless city.' At the galleries he took intense delight in discovering the paintings and sculptures hitherto known to him only in reproductions. He was quite over-whelmed by the Murillo collection in the Louvre,

When I look at them I feel as if I was being touched by a magic wand. It is an experience to be classed along with seeing a performance of *Tristan* or *Zarathustra*, attending the first Weingartner concert in Berlin or hearing Dohnányi play the Beethoven concerto in Vienna this year or catching my first glimpse of the Stephanskirche when I was in Vienna 3 or 4 years ago.

His wonder at the banks of the Seine and at the city's parks and woods was tinged with envy of the Parisian 'who can glory in this sight at any time.' He was particularly entranced by the Parc Monceau with its ingenious and harmonious blend of art and nature — 'a little paradise' — and he had disparaging comparisons to draw with Budapest which he suddenly saw as a bed of petit-bourgeois provincialism.

The insights and revelations of Bartók's visit have remarkable parallels with the Parisian experience of Endre Ady, the foremost Hungarian poet of the period to whom Bartók became attracted a few years later. His *Five Songs for voice and piano, op. 16*, are all settings of Ady poems. At this stage, it seems that Bartók remained unaware of the recent currents and developments in French music which were to profoundly influence his own thinking. In fact, in a letter from Paris to Irmy Jurkovics, he categorically states that,

Bach, Beethoven, Schubert and Wagner have written such quantities of distinctive and characteristic music that all the music of France, Italy and the Slavs combined is as nothing by comparison!

He patriotically puts up a case for Liszt being the one who most closely approaches the 'Big Four', but of Debussy there is no mention. (And what has become of Richard Strauss?)

Irmy Jurkovics and her sister Emsy had become devoted admirers of Bartók since the day of his first public recital in Nagyszentmiklós in 1903, so the tone of his letter is superficially bright and informative, but it does little to conceal his underlying depression. He describes the communication difficulties of the English, Spanish, German, Turkish and American residents of his boarding house with detached amusement, but these anecdotes carry less weight than the problems and anxieties which were troubling him even then. He lays down unequivocally his commitment to atheism, and touches on his flirtation with Nietzschian ideals, a theme which recurs in a serious letter to his mother about family problems written a few week later,

I would recommend to anyone the attempt to achieve a state of spiritiual indifference in which it is possible to view the affairs of the world with complete indifference and with the utmost tranquillity. Of course, it is difficult, extremely difficult — in fact the most difficult thing there is — to attain this state, but success in this is the greatest victory man can ever hope to win: over other people, over himself and over all things.

His style, as usual, is matter of fact, dispassionate, but through it his uncertainty and sense of isolation well up like a cry of despair,

I may be looked after by Dietl or Mandl in Vienna, and I may have friends in Budapest (Thomán, Mrs Gruber), yet there are times when I suddenly become aware of the fact that I am absolutely alone! And I prophesy, I have a foreknowledge, that this spiritual loneliness is to be my destiny.

If the fruits of his French experience lay dormant for a while, the seeds of another far more important influence had already begun to take root. In 1903, in the early days of his nationalist fever, Bartók had written home asking his sister to identify two Hungarian folk tunes. Subsequent research has revealed that the Bartóks had a domestic servant called Lidi Dosa from the Székely region and it was from her that he had picked up these and other melodies. The momentous significance of this chance encounter seems to have eluded him at the time, but to the retrospective onlooker there can be little doubt that it marked the beginning of his true life's work. A more thorough examination of indigenous musical characteristics was an obvious step to take in the furtherance of his avowed intention to serve 'the good of Hungary and the Hungarian nation', but he can have had no inkling of the enormity of the task, nor of the extent to which it was to possess him and direct his entire life. Almost immediately he was aware of the gulf that separated true peasant music, handed down from generation to generation, from popular pseudo-folk-art but it turned out to be wider and more complete than even he had imagined. On the one hand, he discovered,

a natural phenomenon, just like the various forms of the animal or vegetable Kingdom. As a result, its individual organisms — the melodies themselves — are examples of the highest artistic perfection,

on the other,

the usual gypsy slop.

It took him not much longer to realise that interest in his chosen field of dedicated research was practically non-existent. Professed intellectuals, he found, tended to be at once 'not sufficiently naïve but not yet sufficiently educated' to appreciate the scientific and artistic value of such primitive material.

The confusion between popular gypsy-style music and folk music was as well entrenched in Hungary as in the rest of Europe, where the *tzigane* formulae adopted from time to time by composers from Haydn to Liszt was accepted unquestioningly as a reflection of earthy Hungarianism. Liszt himself had produced a long book *On the Gypsies and their Music in Hungary* which gave the myth a

Hungarian peasant life—the source of Bartók's inspiration. (Corvina)

further stamp of authority, although he also expressed a desire to visit the remoter parts of rural Hungary in search of folk material. However, that was never more than a romantic daydream and he never went so far as setting foot in the mud to follow it through. The one dissenting voice, it seems, was a long-forgotten violinist and composer, August von Adelburg (Turkish born, Viennese trained), who challenged Liszt's assumptions in a pamphlet published in 1859 and laboriously entitled 'Reply to Dr Franz Liszt on his assertion in his works that there is no Hungarian national music other than Gypsy music.'

There had been intermittent excursions into the realms of folk-lore by amateur anthropologists throughout the nineteenth century, but, by and large, they had been more concerned with the words than the music of folksong. Such investigation as there had been into folk music had been indiscriminating and unreliable. Even Béla Vikon, who pioneered the use of the phonograph in collecting folksong, was no trained musician and his recordings had to be transcribed by others at a later date. It was Hungary's great good fortune that the two men who rescued and preserved this ancient musical culture for posterity (in the nick of time too, before the explosive expansion of radio and recorded music obliterated it forever) were, in Bartók and Kodály, both meticulous and dedicated scholars as well as composers of genius. Kodály made his first collecting tour in the summer of 1905 (when Bartók was busy with the Rubinstein competition) and in the following year Bartók set off for the Great Hungarian Plains. From a personal point of view, it was a therapeutic venture. Although he had completed his *Suite No. 1* for orchestra during a stay in Vienna following the Parisian débacle, he was heading for another creative impasse. This new passion for folksong research together with performing engagements in Spain and Portugal freed him from any moral obligation to compose for the time being. In fact, his letters suggest he was in rare good humour, making light of, even enjoying the frustrations and absurdities with which the life of the inexperienced traveller is fraught. In Madrid, he and the violin prodigy Ferenc Vecsey were received by the Queen of Spain, who proceeded to trample on Bartók's deepest sensibilities one by one, but his gleeful account of the incident is free of righteous indignation,

My facial muscles were subjected to a severe trial by my efforts not to burst out laughing! She talked a lot of rot, but her prize remark (about Hungary and the Hungarian language) was, 'Your King speaks Hungarian very well, doesn't he? (Old Francis Joe) I agreed, very well. She asked me to play some Hungarian music — czardas. I didn't mind: I let her have her joy. If only she had known what a Hapsburg-hating republican she was speaking to!

1908—collecting folk songs in Darázs, now Drazovce (Czechoslovakia).

Similarly, he is more amused than exasperated by the difficulties in tracking down aged peasants and coaxing songs out of them.

The first tangible result of their labours was a collection of *Twenty Hungarian Folksongs* which Bartók and Kodály published in 1906. It is not wholly characteristic of Bartók's work in this field and was soon withdrawn by the publishers through lack of demand. Nonetheless, it remains an important landmark in the growth of Bartók's personality and of Hungarian music as a living force. It is virtually impossible to over-emphasise the importance of this immersion in folk music in considering any aspect of the composer. His experience with the peasants, an ever-present reminder of the corrupting force of social pretension, formed the basis of his gradual shift from a narrow concept of nationalism to the broad humanitarian ideals of a 'brotherhood of peoples' which imbued his later work and attitudes with the universality which lies at the heart of his greatness.

As for his music, he soon realised that he held in his hands the means to his goal, the raw material of a new, individual and uniquely Hungarian style. In his many lectures, essays and pamphlets on his researches and experiences in the field of folk music, he makes it clear that the features that he painstakingly codified and tabulated were gradually incorporated into his own

31

musical thinking. The first and most important discovery was that most of the melodies were based on scales and modes that had not been used in concert music for centuries, if at all. The prevalence of pentatonic (five-note) scales in turn suggested novel combinations and a whole new system of harmony,

For the majority — and most valuable — of the melodies I collected during my research tours, moved in the old church tonalities, that is, in the Greek and certain other even more primitive (pentatonic) modes, and show the most varied and freely changing metrical and rhythmic patterns performed in both rubato (freely) and 'tempo giusto' (exact time). It is now clear that the ancient scales, that are no longer used in our folk-art music, have lost none of their vitality. Their application has made possible new types of harmonic combinations.

Furthermore,

From this music we may learn unique terseness of expression and inexorable rejection of all inessentials — and that is exactly what we have been longing for after the prolixity of Romanticism.

Eventually, his assimilation of these ideals became so complete that it becomes impossible to say, without foreknowledge, where his thematic material is a genuine folk melody or of his own devising.

Whereas Kodály continued to occupy himself in the main with Hungarian material, Bartók felt compelled to follow up connections with folk music from neighbouring territories, to seek out

Bartók and Kodály.
(Embassy of the Hungarian People's Republic)

32

differences and similarities or to speculate on migratory patterns, and his final tally amounts to many thousands of melodies of Hungarian, Slovak, Rumanian, Bulgarian, Ruthenian, Turkish and even Arabic origin. As Kodály remarked, 'if his interest had turned to money, he would long since have become a millionaire!'

Kodály, 'who guided and advised me in my study of every kind of music,' was also instrumental in introducing the final transitional element in the development of Bartók's mature style — the music of Claude Debussy. Bartók, like musicians throughout Europe, was greatly taken with the novelty, the exotic harmony and colouring of the Frenchman's music, but two other features held a special attraction for him. Firstly, he fancied that he could discern in Debussy's use of simple melodic outlines the very element which appealed to him in Hungarian peasant melody, and, secondly, its utter remoteness from the German mainstream was a virtue in itself. . . .

New ideas were released and the emergence of Debussy signified the replacement of German music by French music as a source of inspiration.

Clearly, if this wealth of new experience was to be exploited to the full in a fresh burst of creative activity, he would have to take steps to reconcile the conflicting demands of his career. In November 1906, he had written to Lajos Dietl in Vienna,

The practising has not been at all to my taste; it's a nuisance and I'd far rather have spent my time collecting as many more songs as possible.

The rigours and time wasting involved in his rôle as a travelling performer were becoming an increasing source of irritation, and, in the summer of 1907, an opportunity arose to instil a measure of stability into his life and at the same time to fulfil an ambition that Paula Bartók had cherished on her son's behalf for some time.

István Thomán was due to retire at the end of the academic year, and on the strength of his recommendation, supported by the director Mihalovich, Bartók was invited to succeed him. He took his teaching duties very seriously, and, like Dohnányi, contributed in no small measure to the stream of outstanding pianists to emerge from Hungary in this century. But like most creative artists he often found the work infuriatingly time-consuming and irksome. Nevertheless, it resolved his problems for the moment and he wrote in his autobiography,

In 1907 I was appointed professor at the Academy of Music and I particularly welcomed this appointment because it gave me an opportunity to settle down at home and pursue my research into folk music.

The Academy of Music, Budapest, where Bartók became a professor of piano in 1907.
(Embassy of the Hungarian People's Republic)

Chapter Four

Before taking up his duties at the Academy, Bartók embarked on another folksong collecting tour, this time in the depths of Transylvania. It was to become a regular pattern in the next few years. During term time he remained, perforce, in Budapest, where his mother joined him in his flat in Teréz Körút, but at least once each year he set off into the country to pursue his obsession and, it seems, to fulfil some spiritual need and seek solace in a natural and 'uncontaminated' existence. 'There is peace among the peasants,' he wrote at the end of his days, 'hatred for their brothers is fostered only by the higher circles.' Painstakingly, though with occasional outbursts of exasperation, he pieced together his collection 'in the parlours of pubs, in bootmakers' workshops, sometimes in the open air.'

A Hungarian village scene around the turn of the century. Children's games provided the titles for many of Bartók's short piano pieces. (Corvina)

He explained some of the difficulties the folklorist could expect to encounter in an article written in 1921,

Nothing is more difficult than the collection of melodies of this kind. We have to look for them among the simplest and poorest peasants, far away from the railroad, if we intend to find material untouched by the contaminating influence of the cities. But it is just these peasants of 'untouched' territories who will usually greet with fierce mistrust the stranger knocking at their door! It is in vain that one tries to explain to them why their old, almost forgotten melodies are being collected; they don't listen to reason. They bestir themselves to attribute the most ridiculous explanations to this strange fact, because they never get to understand why a gentleman from the town would leave his accustomed comfort for the sole reason of hearing them sing their old village tunes. Many of them are totally convinced that this means some extra tax, this time on their music! A certain bashfulness joins this fear: they are nearly always afraid that the gentleman might make fun of their ingenuous and simple melodies. The folklorist, therefore, must have much time and patience to cope with so much mistrust.

In spite of his frustrations and discomforts, this brief summer of 1907 seems to have been one of the happiest periods of his life. Although he was appalled by the living conditions of these simple people, he gladly shared their squalor and as the bonds between him

On a folk song collecting trip with Zoltán Kodály and his wife in 1912. (Corvina)

and his subjects grew closer, his scientific curiosity acquired new dimensions of respect and affection. In later years, he looked back on 'these days spent in the villages among the peasants' as 'the happiest of my life.' He made a good friend of György Gyugyi Péntek, a village carpenter in Körösfö, from whom he ordered a table for his Budapest home.

'Now I'm quite at home with them,' he wrote.

'His home consists of a kitchen and a very small workshop with a leaking roof.'

Many years later, Péntek's son, Ferenc, recalled Bartók as 'a gentle, smiling little man, always in a good humour.'

It is pleasant to record this more or less idyllic interlude, for it was the prelude to one of the most severe personal and emotional crises of a life regularly afflicted with bouts of deep, though rigorously controlled depression. It is unlikely that the full story will ever be known because Bartók himself was such an intensely reticent and private man, and because he inspired such fierce loyalty in his few close friends that they have been reluctant to shed light on the circumstances. At the heart of the matter lay Bartók's deep but thwarted love for the beautiful and talented violinist Stefi Geyer, then aged 19, a pupil of Jenö Hubay at the Academy, who later married the Swiss composer and concert promoter Walter Schulthess and settled in Switzerland. After Bartók's death, as a contribution to Hungarian research on the composer, she released the texts of three letters she had received from him in August and September, 1907, which lay bare the passionate temperament behind the oddly aloof face, often seemingly contemptuous in its defiance, that he presented to the world at large. Despite the considerable volume of correspondence that has come to light (and few twentieth century composers have been so thoroughly researched and documented), Bartók admitted that he was a reluctant correspondent and generally only wrote letters through necessity or obligation. Moreover, he was secretive about his private life and feelings to the point of eccentricity, so Stefi Geyer's gesture is enormously helpful in any attempt to reconcile Bartók's icy manner with the fiery intensity of his music.

The first of the letters is cheerful enough — an amusing account of a tortuous but ultimately successful campaign to wheedle a few songs out of an aged peasant woman, set out in the form of a dramatic dialogue between 'The Traveller' and 'The Woman'. The second letter, ostensibly written in reply to a letter from Stefi, followed just three weeks later. It runs to some four thousand words and is virtually a tract on his philosphy of life and on the very meaning of existence.

That he was hopelessly in love could be deduced from his opening paragraph, especially if one compares its agitated manner

Stefi Geyer—Bartók's unrequited passion for her is reflected in much of his music of the period.

with his normal blandly informative style. He had evidently given an address in Vésztö for her to write to him, and

I caught a cold on Monday, but I've come here all the same. I was rash enough to make the journey on a wild, wet day — and all because, ever since last Sunday, I have been wondering whether your decision to write to me augured good news or bad. Perhaps you were only going to tell me a few jokes? Or had you something more serious to put on paper? Which part of my letter would you have thought about and commented on? These conjectures gave me a headache, I had to do something about it as soon as possible — and there was almost a calamity. Your letter had arrived one day ahead of me, and as I had not told them I was coming, they had already sent it back to the post-office.

His tone becomes altogether weightier when he touches on a reference in her letter to religion.

I was absolutely convinced — although we have never talked about it — that you were 'godfearing'. It wasn't difficult for me to put two and two together. This makes it all the more difficult for me to touch on this subject. I am almost afraid to begin.

But 'begin' he does, and it is almost certainly here that the relationship began to founder. Not content to accept their differences and respect one another's beliefs, he launches into a lengthy, cogently argued vindication of his atheism, his belief in the self-sufficient divinity of Nature and man's control of his own destiny, and pours withering scorn on such concepts as the Immortality of the soul and on the ethics and dogmas of the church in general. The letter is signed

'Greetings from AN UNBELIEVER
(who is more honest than a great many believers).'

If he had hoped to win Stefi's heart by his fearless (if tactless) honesty, then he was clearly disabused of this notion by her reply, although its precise contents are known only in as far as they can be deduced from his third letter, which is perhaps the most poignant document in the entire literature of Bartókiana.

Dear Miss Stefi,
By the time I had finished reading your letter, I was almost in tears — and that, as you can imagine, does not usually happen to me every day. Here is a case of human frailty! I anticipated that you might react like this, yet when you actually did so I was upset. Why couldn't I read your letter with cold indifference? Why couldn't I put it down with a smile of contempt? Why should I be so affected by your reaction? So many 'why's', and I think I must leave you to answer them — provided, of course, that you think them worthy of your consideration.

As he reiterates his fundamental beliefs, it does not seem too fanciful to draw parallels with Beethoven's 'Heiligenstadt Testament' which he set down in the aftermath of his hopeless passion for the Countess Giulietta Guicciardi, dedicatee of his 'Moonlight' Sonata. The precarious emotional equilibrium of the creative artist is similarly expressed.

Beethoven: 'For I have so sensitive a body that even a slight change can transport me from the highest to the most wretched state.'
Bartók: 'One letter from you, a line, even a word — and I am in a transport of joy, the next brings me almost to tears, it hurts so.'

Where Beethoven draws strength from his belief, Bartók

struggles to draw strength from his disbelief. The inner loneliness which he had confided to his mother two years earlier is now more oppressive than ever.

After reading your letter, I sat down at the piano — I have a sad misgiving that I shall never find any consolation in life save in music. And yet. . .

There follow nine bars of mournful music, *Adagio molto*. Above a phrase of four notes he has written, 'this is your *Leitmotif*.'[1]

Consolation in music was what he sought now and in the works which he composed in a steady stream between 1907 and 1911 he gradually achieved the integration of the eclectic and sometimes disparate elements which characterised his output up to this point. He was aiming for a synthesis of the intellectual and structural control of the great classical masters, the novelty and un-German transparency of Debussy and, most importantly, the ancient, primordial elements of Hungarian folk music. His first task was to complete his second orchestral *Suite op. 4* which he had started and abandoned during his stay in Vienna, and the folk element, if mildly expressed, is already clearly to be heard.

He composed a great deal of piano music during this period, much of it for children which may have been a side effect of his teaching involvement at the Academy or more often it seems, a convenient and less arduous medium in which to try out his new ideas. In 1931, he attempted to categorise the methods by which folksong can be 'transmuted' into modern music. The first possibility, he said, was to leave the original melody virtually intact, but to lavish the utmost thought and feeling on how best to highlight its unique characteristics by means of an illuminating accompaniment or by adding an introduction and conclusion. He likened this technique to that of a jeweller fixing a precious stone in its setting. Perhaps the most perfect examples in this category are the 4 volumes *For Children*, 85 enchanting settings of Hungarian and Slovak folktunes which have taken their place alongside Bach's *Anna Magdalena Notebook* and Schumann's *Album for the Young* as a cornerstone of the child's repertoire.

The *Fourteen Bagatelles* are another matter. Often blatantly experimental, sometimes sketchy in detail, they represent decisive steps towards the future and many of the traits of Bartók's mature style can be discerned in embryonic form. In June, 1908, Bartók played them to Busoni who exclaimed, 'At last! Something *really* new.' Busoni, a tireless champion of new music, tried to interest his

---

1. *Leitmotif* (German) Musical term denoting a single short phrase or even a single chord that is constantly associated with a particular character or event (most notably used by Wagner in his music dramas).

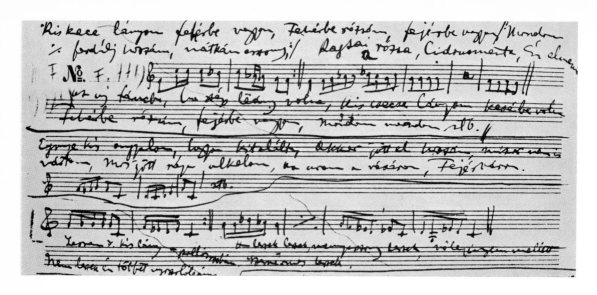

A Hungarian folk song sketch which was the basis of one of the piano pieces 'For Children'.

own publishers, the prestigious German firm Breitkopf and Härtel, in them but they timidly rejected them as 'too difficult and modern for the public.' Busoni also invited Bartók to conduct the Scherzo from his Suite No. 2 in Berlin the following year, a novel and exhilarating (if nerve-racking) experience which he never repeated.

Busoni's support was welcome, as words of appreciation and understanding were hard to come by. Etelka Freund, a former pupil, was another patient propagandist on Bartók's behalf and it was thanks to her advocacy that the distinguished Swiss (later American) pianist Rudolph Ganz became one of the first to include Bartók's music in his programme. Bartók was appreciative, and wrote to Ganz

Your kind lines (just received) have given me real pleasure, especially as I have had to endure an unbelievable number of attacks all provoked by these very piano pieces . . . hardly more than one in a hundred will find any pleasure in these works, and I have to be thankful if they are not labelled as products of frenzy or insanity as has often occurred.

He was particularly stung by the remark of the eminent German musicologist, Hugo Leichtentritt who, after attending the Berlin performance of the orchestral *Scherzo*, declared that Bartók 'had no clear notion of the essential requirements necessary to give artistic significance to a composition.'

Happily, such setbacks did not this time stem the flow of inspiration, as had Koessler's grumpy antipathy in his student days, for he was confident that he was on the right path. Performances of his orchestral works, while neither a regular nor frequent feature of the Budapest Philharmonic season, were becoming accepted as occasional events of some importance, even if the standard of

40

performance left much to be desired. Although they were invariably greeted with a more or less equal mixture of cheers and catcalls, Bartók was far from dismayed by this reaction, and even felt sufficiently encouraged to compose further orchestral works. In fact, this mixture of adulatory enthusiasm and hostility was becoming the norm for important premières of those composers who were blazing their respective trails away from the comfortable opulence of late romanticism. Schoenberg, Berg, Hindemith and Prokofiev all had similar experiences and the trend reached its zenith in the notorious riots which attended the Paris première of Stravinsky's ballet *The Rite of Spring* in 1913. Peter Ustinov coined the memorable phrase, a 'fiasco d'estime', which neatly suggests a certain *cachet* which attached to the composer on such occasions.

The very title *Two Pictures* for orchestra op. 10 calls to mind Debussy and his *Images* for piano and for orchestra, and the first of these reveals the influence of the French master more strongly than any of Bartók's other orchestral works. The second, a stamping rustic dance, has, in addition, a new earthiness in its handling of folk material.

A further orchestral work, *Two Portraits (One Ideal, One Grotesque)* op. 5 assumed a peculiar interest in the light of the Stefi Geyer letters. In the summer of 1907, Bartók started work on a two-movement violin concerto for Stefi. Although Bartók scholars had known of its existence for many years, it was not performed during the composer's lifetime, and the complete score only came to light among Stefi Geyer's effects after her death in 1956. However, the first movement of the concerto, serenely meditative but for its soaring impassioned climax, turned out to be none other than the first *Portrait* (*The Ideal*), and its thematic base is clearly the 'leitmotif' in the third letter to Stefi. The second, 'grotesque' *Portrait* is an orchestral version of the last of the *Fourteen Bagatelles* for piano, a shrill, hysterical 'Danse Macabre' in which the themes of the 'ideal' portrait are twisted and distorted with strident irony. This scheme is of special fascination to musicologists because Liszt used exactly the same technique in his *Faust Symphony*, where the themes of the Faust movement are grotesquely disfigured to express the evil spirit of negation in the Mephistopheles movement. The last two *Bagatelles*, a lugubrious dirge and this frantic waltz which became the second portrait, are both shot through with the melancholy strains that Bartók jotted down in the letter. According to Denijs Dille, the Flemish researcher, Stefi Geyer severed her relations with Bartók in February, 1908, and the Bagatelles were completed shortly afterwards. So the psychological inferences of this pair of portraits are even more thought-provoking than the musicological ones.

Other piano works, the *Two Rumanian Dances*, *Two Elegies*, *3*

Burlesques (op. 8a, b and c), the *Four Dirges* and the *Seven Sketches* (op. 9a and b), all composed between 1908 and 1910, show notable advances along the 'new road', although Bartók's sporadic lapses into a Lisztian piano style sometimes sit uneasily with his growing terseness of expression. The only chamber work in this sustained creative burst was the *String Quartet No. 1, op. 8,* intense, serious and moving and an important work in its own right, but more especially so as the first in a series of six quartets that have become accepted without argument as true classics of 20th century music. When Kodály said that it concerned 'a man's return to life after travelling to the very borders of non-existence,' he was evidently referring to his knowledge that Bartók had actually contemplated suicide over the Stefi Geyer affair.

In a memorial speech, Kodály described his friend's driving force as 'a thirst for knowledge, perseverance, love of work and a consuming interest in all forms of musical expression.' In connection with his work at the Academy, Bartók took on an additional burden in starting a series of editorial revisions of a wide range of keyboard music. This immersion in baroque and classical music was no doubt the source of a final external influence on his music, although its effects are not really to be felt until some years later.

Among his class at the Academy were two sisters, Herma and Marta Ziegler, daughters of an inspector in the police force. It is clear that Bartók soon formed a particular attachment for the younger girl, Marta, for he dedicated the *Portrait of a Girl* in his *Seven Sketches* to her in 1908. Just how close they had become was suspected by no-one apparently, and the ensuing events reveal that Bartók's mania for privacy had reached almost comic proportions. Jenö Kerpely, 'cellist in the Waldbauer-Kerpely Quartet which was closely associated with Bartók, related the bizarre tale after he had emigrated to America many years later. The sixteen-year-old Marta was having her lesson at Bartók's home one morning in the autumn of 1909, and Bartók told his mother that she would be staying for lunch. The lesson continued into the afternoon and Paula Bartók raised her eyebrows enquiringly on being told, 'Marta will stay to supper, too.' Only then did Bartók grudgingly add, 'We're married.' They continued to keep their marriage a secret from the outside world for a while until Marta absent-mindedly referred to the professor as 'my husband.' The cat was out of the bag and Dohnányi immediately sent them a congratulatory telegram, which Bartók hotly resented as an intrusion into his private affairs!

Bartók's insatiable appetite for work was not diminished by this change in his domestic circumstances. His folk music researches continued unabated and his young wife often accompanied him on

Bartók, Kodály and the members of the Waldbauer-Kerpely String Quartet—the phalanx of the musical avant-garde in Budapest.

his tours. They were fortunate in having Paula Bartók on hand to help in caring for young Béla junior, who was born in August, 1910. There were occasional and much acclaimed concert appearances in popular concertos by Liszt and Saint-Saëns, but from this time onwards, Bartók was really only interested in playing his own music in public.

Two especially noteworthy concerts took place in Budapest and Paris in 1909 and 1910 respectively. At the local event, the brilliant young Waldbauer-Kerpely Quartet (whose oldest member was twenty-five years old, the youngest a mere eighteen) played the first quartets of both Bartók and Kodály which once more aroused the antagonism of the establishment but caused great excitement amongst the burgeoning avant-garde circle. The mouthpiece of progressive intellectuals was a literary magazine of great vitality, *Nyugat* (West), founded by the liberal writer Hugo Ignotus, to which Endre Ady was a leading contributor. Its aims as expressed by Ignotus's son Paul, in his masterly study 'Hungary' (London 1972), were precisely those of Bartók himself,

The *Nyugat* guard were determined to create a totally European Hungary, delivered from parochialism; but, at the same time, to assert the national

43

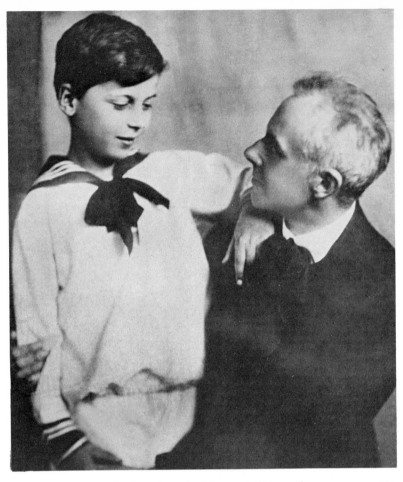

Bartók with his three year old son Béla jnr. in the garden of the house in Rakoskerestúr. (Embassy of the Hungarian People's Republic)

Béla Balázs—librettist of *The Wooden Prince* and *Duke Bluebeard's Castle*.

personality and to dig deep into the Magyar heritage of images, concepts, and melodies, and refurbish what had been debased by usage and foreign influences,

so he would have found the perceptive and enthusiastic reviews of Géza Csáth, the magazine's lively young music critic, particularly heart-warming.

The 'Festival Hongrois' presented in Paris the following year by Sándor Kovfács, included music by Léo Weiner, Árpád Szendy, Ödön Mihalovich and Dohnányi, as well as by the two modernists, Bartók and Kodály who were branded in the press as 'young barbarians'. Bartók's reply was his *Allegro Barbaro* for piano, a piece of even greater ferocity than anything he had previously produced. It is typical of a certain strain in his music, evoking the primitive violence and indomitable rhythmic energy that delighted him in peasant dances; but it was unfortunate that this single aspect of his work was seized upon by critics of delicate sensibility who could see in him nothing more than a brutal, savage iconoclasm.

'Tonal chaos arising from the diabolical employment of

unrelated keys simultaneously,' is typical of the sort of criticism he
had to endure for most of his career.

Despite the defiant gestures, there were signs that Bartók's
resolve was beginning to crumble; small wonder, when we consider
that he had been working at white heat for more than three years
only to have inched forward to a position precariously balanced
between neglect and notoriety. Antal Molnár, the violist in the
Waldbauer-Kerpely Quartet and a new recruit to folk music
research, described Bartók's withdrawal,

He spoke as matter-of-factly as a locksmith showing his tools to a new
apprentice, but with flattering brevity. Otherwise he stared at me with
wide questioning eyes, quite often for fifteen minutes at a time.

It was Béla Balázs, poet, novelist and dramatist, who conjured
one last gigantic effort out of Bartók,

I talked to him about the great Hungarian renaissance, the necessity for a
Hungarian contribution to the development of European culture, and I

45

encouraged him. . . . But I had never before observed in anyone the tight lips and unchanging deathly pallor with which Béla Bartók listened to me.

Thus Bartók, with Balázs as librettist, embarked upon his first and only opera *Duke Bluebeard's Castle*. Although the source of the one-act scenario was the age-old legend of the murderous Bluebeard and his seven wives, the psycho-analytic approach of composer and librettist is a far cry from the blood and thunder of nineteenth-century operatic melodrama. The critic, Sándor Veress described its theme as 'the eternal tragedy of the dualism of man and woman, the heavenly and earthly perspective of their souls.' Of more significance to Bartók, surely, was the impenetrable loneliness of Bluebeard, inescapably bound by his own nature, from which he cannot be free even by the total self-sacrifice of the woman, Judith. The music, while clearly influenced by Debussy's *Pelleas et Melisande* is a brilliant kaleidoscope of sound imagery and psychological nuance (Stefi Geyer's *leitmotif* is unmistakeably present), but the lack of dramatic stage action betrays the libretto's poetic origins and makes severe demands on the audience's attention.

In a despairing effort to improve the performing standards and general climate for contemporary music, an attempt was made to set up a *New Hungarian Music Society* (*UMZE*), but it ran into one obstacle after another. Before long, Bartók was scribbling furiously on a postcard to Etelka Freund,

This UMZE has been such a nuisance that I would like to consign it to the depths of hell.

Duke Bluebeard's Castle was rejected out of hand in a competition organised by the Lipótvárosi Kaszinó, and the two failures were too much for Bartók, who now gave up the struggle and withdrew from public life. He was still smarting with frustration eighteen months later, when he wrote explaining his reasons to Géza Vilmos Zágan, a colleague who had worked hard in the cause of modern music,

. . . a year ago sentence of death was passed on me as a composer. Either those people are right, in which case I am an untalented bungler; or I am right, and it's they who are the idiots. In either event, this means that between myself and them (that is, our musical leaders: Hubay, etc.) there can be no discussion of music, still less any joint action . . . Therefore I have resigned myself to write for my writing-desk only.

But one flame was not extinguished,

My public appearances are confined to *one sole field*: I will do anything to further my research work in musical folklore.

46

Chapter Five

In the years leading to the first world war the political scene in Hungary had become a farrago of ever-increasing complexity, in which conflicting ideals and vested interests jostled to produce a series of dramatic changes and gestures that were so frequent and impermanent as to result in stalemate. The fundamental obstacles to political maturity (in a present-day sense) would seem to be clear enough — the continuing dependence on Vienna and a restricted franchise. However, these issues were clouded by the reluctance of the various factions to concede their present positions of power — the gentry over the peasantry, the Magyars over the ethnic minorities and the Hapsburgs over all. Although implacably opposed to one another, the active partisans of each power *bloc* were secretly in dread of a genuine popular uprising, and each exploited the others' fear of it. The parties strove to reconcile their conflicting objectives with a startling degree of compromise and often with disregard for logic. Magyar supremacy could be equated with the power of the gentry over the peasantry, hence we find radical intellectuals leaning towards the dynastic camp as their best means of undermining aristocratic wealth and privilege. On the other hand, pillars of the landowning establishment emerged as champions of the common man in retaliation against Hapsburg attempts to clip their wings. The heir to the Imperial throne, the dour and pedantic Prince Franz Ferdinand, was perceptive enough to see the possible advantage in these anomalies, and for a while tightened the Hapsburg grip by granting minor concessions to the opposed sectional interests. But his manner in doing so, together with his charmless personality, succeeded only in antagonising *en bloc* the disparate elements in Hungarian society. In any event, history was against him, for where he had hoped to win support from Romanov Russia and Imperial Britain, hindsight tells us that the Republican movements in France and Italy were more relevant to the Hungarian situation.

The universal distaste for Franz Ferdinand felt by almost every shade of Hungarian opinion makes it the more absurd and inexplicable that the nation's leaders and press should have joined so loudly in the clamour for war that followed his assassination at Sarajevo on

1918—with his friends Ion Buşiţiă and Zoltán Kodály.

June 28, 1914. On the face of it, the idea of avenging a Hapsburg could scarcely have been further removed from the mood of the Hungarian people. Paul Ignotus could only explain it as 'a general malaise from which everyone tried to escape into military adventure.'

Bartók's interest in the squabbles of party politics was minimal. He had made his anti-Hapsburg sentiments clear long ago, but by now his Hungarianism was tempered by his affection for the minority races, especially Slovak and Romanian, with whom he had become involved on his collecting tours. He was moving away from 'a narrow, parochial nationalism towards his ideal of a 'brotherhood of nations'. He had no taste for sabre-rattling and was deeply shocked by the suddenness of the catastrophe.

I have been so upset by world events that my mind has been almost completely paralysed,

he wrote in September, 1914.

He was not called for military service on medical grounds (he weighed only 98 pounds), but his mood of depression and introversion was not helped by the additional threat to his collecting activities. When he did venture out, however, he found that things were not so bad as he feared — for the time being, at least.

It is hard to imagine that anyone could go on collecting folk-songs in times like these. But it can be done. The amazing thing is that you can do it exactly as in peace-time. The peasants are so merry and lighthearted, one might think they don't care a rap about the war.

The collection was growing apace, and by the end of the war he had amassed some 1,000 Hungarian, Romanian, Slovak, Bulgarian, Ruthenian, Serbian, even Arabic folksongs. With Kodály's help he began to classify this mass of material, using a modified form of the system devised by the Finnish folklorist, Ilmari Krohn.

His original compositions between 1910 and 1915 are sparse indeed, and the bulk of his output from this time is derived from the Romanian material he had started to gather in 1909. There are many treasures to be found here, including the enchanting *Sonatina* for piano and the *Six Romanian Folk Dances*, one of his most popular works which has undergone further rearrangement for almost every conceivable instrument. An examination of his original precise transcript of what the peasant musicians actually played him on their strange violins, flutes and bagpipes reveals the subtlety and delicacy with which the definitive piano version imprints his own personal and unifying style on their exotic

48

Below left Marta and Paula
Bartók, 1915.
(Embassy of the Hungarian
People's Republic)

Bartók during his years of
seclusion.

nuances and mannerisms, rendering them alive and intelligible to
the concert performer, or to the sympathetic amateur.

Bartók formed close and lasting friendships as a result of these
Romanian sorties, notably with Ion Buşitia, a schoolmaster of many
talents, who lent wholehearted support and companionship to his
projects. He was rewarded with a niche in posterity by Bartók's
dedication of the *Six Romanian Dances*. Another Romanian contact,
the conductor Dumitru Kiriac laid a significant milestone in
Bartók's career by arranging the publication (Bucharest, 1913) of
the first of his many ethno-musicological monographs, a lesser-
known side of the composer's output which gives fascinating
insights into his own musical language.

Bartók was fully aware that this surprisingly tranquil and
trouble-free situation could not continue indefinitely.

Budapest Opera House where the first two stage works were produced.

My long silence has been due to the fact that every now and then I am thrown into a state of deep depression by the war, (he wrote to Ion Buşiţia in May, 1915) a condition which, in my case, alternates with a kind of devil-may-care attitude. In all my thinking there is a *ceterum censeo*: nothing matters, but to remain friends with Romania; it would be a grievous thing to me to see my beloved Transylvania devastated, besides greatly hindering my prospect of finishing, or rather continuing, my work. In fact, I can't hold out much hope for work of this kind; the future seems gloomy indeed!

His fears were well founded. In August, 1916, Romania invaded the Transylvanian territory of Hungary. Marta Bartók and young Béla were in the region at the time and for three weeks Bartók waited in an agony of suspense for word whether they were alive or dead.

As the war tightened its grip on the country, remorselessly isolating his research territory, Bartók returned to his writing desk, and several important works now flowed from his pen. The bleak desolation of the fourth movement of his *Suite, op. 14* for piano suggests a deserted battlefield, while in the ferocious, whirlwind

50

third movement, the Arabic scales implanted in Bartók's mind during his visit to Biskra (North Africa) in 1913 emerge for the first time. The passionate and moving *String Quartet No. 2*, composed at the same time concludes in a similar manner: subsiding into eerie stillness, its fury spent in the barbarous Second movement.

Two song cycles followed, Bartók's only contribution to the *genre*, if we except student efforts and the numerous folksong arrangements. The *Five Songs, op. 16* are settings of poems by Endry Ady, far and away the leading Hungarian poet of the time and *doyen* of the *Nyugat* radicals. The *Five Songs, op. 15* are of more curious origin. For many years, their texts were given as 'by unknown author(s)', but research in Hungary has shown them to be the work of sixteen-year-old Klara Gombossy, a forester's daughter who accompanied Bartók on several collecting expeditions. Their friendship lasted about a year, and the fact that her authorship is not credited on the score has given rise to speculation that their relationship may have been deliberately kept secret.

But the most exciting event of the war years was undoubtedly the production of the one-act ballet *The Wooden Prince*; not for posterity, perhaps, for it has never received the same recognition outside Hungary as Bartók's other stage works (*Duke Bluebeard's Castle* and *The Miraculous Mandarin*), but because it provided the composer with his first taste of unqualified public success and acclaim. The libretto, again by Bela Balázs, was published in *Nyugat* in 1913, a naïve fairy-tale of a princess who spurns the ardent prince in favour of the wooden puppet he creates for her, but

Below right Scene from *The Wooden Prince*.
Below left Scene from *Duke Bluebeard's Castle*.
(Embassy of the Hungarian People's Republic)

Egisto Tango—the Italian conductor and saviour of *The Wooden Prince*.

decked out with elaborate symbolism that today smacks of archness or pretentiousness at times. Bartók was taken by the idea of art (the puppet) being made a rich girl's plaything at the expense of the artist's feelings, but he also wanted to show, by setting a second libretto by Balázs, his faith in their previous collaboration, the rejected *Duke Bluebeard's Castle*. He had started work on the score in 1913, and now, in his latest surge of creative vitality, took it up again. The project was fraught with every kind of obstacle. No Hungarian conductor would touch it, the orchestra said it was unplayable and the ballet master (who understood not a note of the music) pronounced it undanceable as well. Anxious well-wishers advised cancellation to avoid a certain fiasco.

Bartók himself would probably have thrown in the towel, retreating into a fit of righteous indignation reminiscent of his Paris experience.

What is the Royal Opera House anyway?! An Augean stable; a dumping ground for every kind of rubbish; the seat of all disorder; the pinnacle of confusion.

But all was not lost. The dynamic Italian conductor Egisto Tango demanded (and got) no less than thirty rehearsals and Balázs himself took over the coaching of the corps de ballet. Their enthusiasm and dedication infected the whole company, and when the curtain came down after the first performance on May 12, 1917, the doubters were confounded. Balázs recalls that 'the applause broke out in the galleries, and like an avalanche swept down to the boxes and the stalls, carrying before it all the rabble of the press. Many reviews had to be rewritten that night.' Bartók, Balázs and Tango were recalled to the stage fifteen times. In deepest gratitude for 'a musically perfect performance' Bartók dedicated the score to Egisto Tango. The depression and pangs of rejection were lifted for a while. The autobiography reads,

The year 1917 brought a change in the attitude of the Budapest public toward my compositions, I had the wonderful luck to hear a major work of mine, a ballet entitled *The Wooden Prince*, performed in a perfect manner under the direction of Maestro Egisto Tango. In 1918 he also arranged a performance of an older work of mine, *Duke Bluebeard's Castle*.

On a darker note he goes on,

After these promising beginnings there followed, alas! the complete political and economic breakdown of 1918. The sad and troubled times that followed for about a year and a half were not conducive to serious work.

52

Chapter Six

While Bartók was absorbed in *The Wooden Prince*, the seeds of the collapse had already taken root. As the war dragged on, the spurious bellicosity stirred up at the outset gave way to frustration, boredom and misery. The political manoeuvring and sniping of the pre-war years became increasingly bitter and recriminatory, and by the time the conflict approached its messy and ragged conclusion the hostility between the various shades of authoritarians, democrats and communists was at boiling point. Scapegoats for the deprivation and humiliation of the wasted years were sought by all sides. For a brief spell it looked as though firm but moderate diplomacy might save the day. The disintegration of the Hapsburg empire into some pattern of national units was a foregone conclusion by the summer of 1918, and within days of the German surrender a Hungarian National Council was set up — in effect an alliance of the old Independence Party and assorted leftish groups from outside parliament. It was headed by Count Mihály (Michael) Károlyi, an immensely wealthy landowner but a man with genuine democratic aspirations, for all his inbred aristocratic *hauteur*. The prime minister, Count István Tisza, made frantic last minute concessions in parliament on practically every contentious issue. But it was too late to stem the flood of support for Károlyi's National Council on which people hysterically pinned their hopes for 'peace' and 'people's welfare'. So Count Tisza, who had been in and out of office since the turn of the century through his skill in the art of compromise, was himself cast as scapegoat and summarily shot in his own home in what was otherwise a surprisingly bloodless *coup*.

But it was a false dawn. Although Károlyi's Council achieved the transition from Imperial satellite to Republic, it could not withstand the vengeful dismemberment of the country by her neighbours in collusion with the victorious powers. In panic, the country lurched to the left in the hope that Lenin's new Soviet Russia would support its territorial claims. A new Hungarian Republic of Councils was formed between two workers' parties under the leadership of the communist agitator Béla Kun who had been hastily released from prison. Economic conditions had sunk

Proclamation of Karolyi's
Republic, 1919.
(Embassy of the Hungarian
People's Republic)

even below wartime levels and the shortage in the cities of basic
commodities like fuel and foodstuffs was aggravated by the influx of
trainloads of refugees from the lost territories. Barely four months
elapsed before the inept adventures of Kun's Red Army opened the
capital to Romanian invaders and yet another junta, this time of a
vicious right-wing militarism. A communist witch-hunt ensued,
involving the indiscriminate slaughter of workers, Jews and
peasants and in March, 1920, Rear Admiral Miklós Horthy,
'Supreme Commander of the Hungarian National Army' was
officially 'elected' head of state, a position he occupied for the rest
of Bartók's life. The series of events was not, indeed, 'conducive to
serious work' and its repercussions were to be felt repeatedly over
the next two decades.

As a state institution, the Academy was not immune from the
shuffling of official positions inevitably associated with these rapid
changes. When Ödön Mihalovich retired as director at the
beginning of 1919, the Károlyi administration appointed Dohnányi
to succeed him with Kodály as his deputy. When the Horthy
régime took effective control in the summer, Dohnányi was abroad
on a concert tour. He returned to Budapest in November to find
himself suspended for one year 'while his appointment was being
reconsidered.' Kodály, Imre Waldbauer the violinist and Kerpely

the 'cellist were also excluded, pending investigation of their activities under the communist government. Bartók himself had been enlisted onto the Music Committee set up by the Kun régime along with Dohnányi and Kodály, but had undertaken no active political rôle apart from his support for Kodály's radical programme of educational reform. His main interest had been in a projected Museum of Music with himself as director of the folk music section (a post he had long dreamed of as an alternative to teaching). At first, he found the bickering little more than a tiresome farce. He pointed out in a letter to his mother that the suspended teachers

continue to draw full salaries, of course, only do no work. In fact, they come off better than those teachers against whom no action has been taken.

He underestimated the situation. Far from fizzling out, as Bartók predicted, the right wing backlash took an uglier turn the following year.

The Horthy government's choice for the post of director was Jenö Hubay, the eminent violinist and teacher, whose dazzling array of pupils included Stefi Geyer, Ferenc Vecsey, Imre Waldbauer, József Szigeti, Jelly Aranyi and Zoltán Székely, all of whom were closely associated with Bartók at some stage in his career. Hubay had presumably satisfied the authorities that he was amenable to political pressure and, as an administrator, he was given to making airy and sweeping pronouncements to the press without consulting his colleagues. Bartók, who was on a six month sabbatical at the time, viewed his elevation with some cynicism from the start,

Mr Hubay has made his triumphal entry into the halls of the National Academy of Music (probably to a festive march composed by himself) . . . he is handing out statements left and right.

By now it was clear that the 'white purge' was not going to blow over and, although Hubay made friendly overtures to Dohnányi and Bartók in his public statements, they were viewed with some caution. Béla Reinitz, the composer who had chaired the Music Committee of the Republic of Councils, was now in prison and Béla Balázs, an avowed communist, had fled the country. What actually spurred Bartók into action was the implementation by a government commission of the long-threatened disciplinary action against his friend Kodály, who was accused, firstly, of being a member of Reinitz's Music Committee and secondly, in his rôle of deputy director of the Academy, of permitting the *Internazionale* to be orchestrated, allowing recruitment of students by the Red Army, and various petty infringements of bureaucratic red tape.

Ernst von Dohnányi—an early victim of the post-war political intrigues.

Bartók and Dohnányi leapt publicly to his aid. Bartók pointed out that, since he too had sat on the same committee, it was flagrantly unjust to single Kodály out for this 'offence', while Dohnányi declared that anything that had occurred during his directorship of the Academy was his responsibility alone. To the charge of 'unpatriotically' collecting folksongs of the minority 'alien' races, Kodály was eloquent in his own defence,

I have never meddled in everyday politics. But figuratively speaking, every bar of music, every folk tune I have recorded has been a political act. In my opinion, that is true patriotism; a policy of actual deeds, not of mere slogans.

Before long, the Ministry officials let the case drop rather than allow the wave of sympathy for Kodály grow into anything more menacing, but not before they had demoted him from deputy director to rank and file teacher.

The persecution of his friend had sinister implications for Bartók, with his close personal and scientific ties with the Romanians and Slovaks. This side of his work ('as necessary to me as fresh air is to other people') had come to an indefinite halt through the curbs on free travel imposed in the wake of the war, and in other respects his future was uncertain, too. The museum post he hankered after had progressed no further than discussions and a more recent suggestion to make him director of the Opera filled him with horror. His exasperation with the cultural authorities was aggravated by a report in a right wing newspaper that he was to sit on a newly appointed Music Council. He immediately sent a stiff note to the Editor-in-chief,

. . . I feel obliged to inform you that, on the contrary, I have received no official approach in this matter; nor would I wish to be a member of any musical council from which the greatest musicians of the country (i.e. Dohnányi and Kodály) are excluded.

Many of his friends and colleagues had fled abroad to escape the purge, and Bartók himself gave serious thought to the possibility of emigrating. Berlin, Vienna, Transylvania and even London were all considered for one reason or another. He had recently signed a contract with the enterprising Universal Edition of Vienna for his music and he now sent some of his ethnographical studies to Germany in the hope of finding an outlet for his growing accumulation of unpublished findings.

In February, 1920, some concert engagements gave him the chance to test the water in Berlin, where he stayed for two months. Postal services had still not been resumed between Hungary and

56

Romania, so it was also a good opportunity to get in touch again with his friend Ion Buşiţia,

At home the outlook is pretty bleak; I have come here to have a look around and see what may be done. I have been pleased to find that I am greatly respected here. At any rate, it would be possible for me to settle here.

Rumours, apparently well founded, reached Budapest that Max Reinhardt had approached Bartók with a view to commissioning a score for his production of *Lysistrata*, and mutterings of 'treachery' were heard in the chauvinist press. In the end, it was his passion for folksong which 'drew him east', as he put it to Buşiţia, and in May he returned to Budapest, not to the little house on Rákoskerestúr where the family had lived for ten years, but to a handsome and spacious mansion in Gyoparutca at the invitation of a benevolent friend, József Lukács (the father of the Marxist philosopher György Lukács). They had only two rooms, but Bartók's sick leave and the ravages of inflation and currency problems had wrought havoc with his finances and they were grateful for this refuge where they remained for about two years.

They had barely settled in when rumblings in the press over Bartók's dealings in Germany erupted into a violent and malicious personal onslaught. The bitterness engendered by the final humiliation of Hungary at the Treaty of Trianon incited the chauvinist elements almost to hysteria, and Bartók found himself branded as a traitor for his findings on, of all things 'The Romanian Folk music Dialect of Hunyad'. The opening salvo was fired by one Professor Elemér Sereghy in the newspaper *Nemzeti Ujsag*. The article was dismissive and insulting about the scientific validity of Bartók's work, but the arguments sprang from political bigotry and hinged on Bartók's 'motives' for attributing Romanian ancestry to material collected within Hungary. It may be that Sereghy's rage was inflamed by the knowledge that Bartók's intermediary in negotiations with German publishers on the essay in question was Géza Révész, a communist refugee from the new régime. A further polemic appeared a few days later, in which Bartók's essay was described as 'treacherous poison' and Kodály as his 'evil genius'. At first, Bartók was content to ignore this catchpenny journalism as irrelevant to any serious discussion of the points at issue. But when Jenö Hubay entered the fray, his voice, with the authority of his position behind it, could not go unchallenged.

Hubay was aware of Bartók's growing international prestige and generally anxious to preserve civil, if not cordial relations with him. But in this matter he found it more prudent to toe the party line and, accordingly, he issued one of his lofty statements to the press.

He deplored the untimely publication of the essay in a German magazine and thought it 'culpable for us to be in any way concerned with the culture of our minorities.' After sweeping condemnation of Bartók's conclusions, he ended with a burst of jingoism that was as stupid as it was shameless.

These questions must not today be judged from a scholarly point of view, but only from that of the national interest of Hungary, which at the present time is, in any event, more important than details of scholarship to which in general no great significance can be ascribed.

Bartók replied with icy fury, refuting the charges one by one.

I read with amazement in today's issue of *Szozat* that director Hubay has identified himself with the charges brought against me by *Nemzeti Ujsag*. I am therefore compelled to reply publicly and point to the most conspicuous examples of those charges which show ignorance, malevolence, and deliberate distortion. . . . The publication of my article was also desirable in order to show those abroad in what high esteem we hold our minorities, the extent of our concern for their cultural matters, how little we oppress them. Or does Hungary's interest possibly not require that we refute our enemies' charge that we oppress our minorities?

After reiterating his belief in his scientific methods and conclusions, he throws down his challenge to Hubay.

Because I have been doing research for more than a decade, I may be less prone to 'errors' than Director Hubay, who — so far as I know — is not acquainted with my Hungarian and other collections, nor has he ever taken any interest in them. If he insists upon his statement, then let him state which of the 'falsified' melodies he considered to be of Romanian origin and he should prove that they are indeed so.

For the moment, the campaign withered in the face of such unshakeable moral conviction. Bartók was contemptuous rather than bitter about it all and gratified that his true friends rallied round him.

I have no cause for complaint against my compatriots either (he wrote to Busitia). Some of them may not have acted fairly towards me; but others have tried to make up for this with all the more zeal.

Although he only reluctantly involved himself with political squabbles of this nature, he was a shrewd judge of shifting trends.

The dictatorship of the military is crushing the intellectual life of the country, just as the dictatorship of the proletariat crushed its economic existence before, he wrote in 1920, and he was perceptive enough to discern even then signs of the canker that was to poison the fabric of Hungarian society.

Far from being censored for the loss of Tango, (another casualty of political intrigue), or for the present inartistic regime, Emil Ábrányi, the general director of the Opera, has merely been accused of possessing too little-marked a sense of 'Christian Nationalism'! He was, in all seriousness, accused of having engaged several new Jewish members and of having performed two local works by Jewish composers. For with us at present it is no longer a question of whether an artist, a singer, a savant is of good repute in his especial class of work, but whether he is a Jew or a man of liberal tendencies. For these two sections of humanity are to be excluded so far as possible from all public activity.

And how did Bartók's own creative force withstand the pressures of this chaotic and frustrating era? Unsurprisingly, his output was sporadic, but the works he did produce show no wavering in the ever-increasing mastery of style and intensity of expression achieved during the war years. Remorselessly he stripped away the familiar and traditional elements that remained and moved towards an uncompromisingly 'modern' idiom, never abandoning his folk sources but moving decisively into the main vanguard of twentieth century European music where his rightful position was increasingly recognised.

Melchior Lengyel, librettist of *The Miraculous Mandarin*, later a Hollywood script writer.

The unexpected success of *The Wooden Prince*, and the emergence at its première of a fervent and vociferous coterie of supporters, encouraged Bartók to stay with the theatre for his next major work, the ballet, or *pantomime grotesque*, *The Miraculous Mandarin*. The lurid and bloody scenario was a far cry from Balázs' poetic and philosophical abstractions, and its author Menyhért (Melchior) Lengyel belonged to the new group of naturalistic writers associated with the Gay Theatre in Budapest. The script was published in *Nyugat* in 1917 and the composer and librettist were introduced over Sunday lunch at István Thomán's house the following year. The taste for horror and atrocity which had entered the world of literature around the turn of the century in the writings of Poe, Wedekind and Wilde was reflected in music by Debussy's projected (though never completed) setting of Poe's *The Fall of the House of Usher* and Strauss's *Salome* (based on Oscar Wilde's play) which had greatly excited Bartók during his Strauss fever. The apocalyptic horrors of the war provoked a fresh wave of literary shockers, and there may have been an element of opportunism in Lengyel's choice of subject. After his fall from grace in Hungary, he successfully adapted his talents to the requirements of Hollywood, where the Garbo classic *Ninotchka* was amongst his many screen credits. Bartók's reasons for choosing the libretto are harder to assess. He was, of course, not unmoved by the ugliness of war, nor was he unaware of current trends in music and literature. He was keenly interested in the music of Stravinsky and Schoenberg and he berated the Hungarian musical establishment for their indifference to important new developments. Marta and he had been working hard at the piano duet arrangement of Stravinsky's *The Rite of Spring* which he saw as a Russian manifestation of the same primordial force that he found in the peasant music of his own land. His own style was moving towards an apex of dissonance and uncompromising harshness which may have been influenced by external factors but also, in terms of his total output, seems evolutionary and inevitable. The elemental passions of *The Miraculous Mandarin* therefore presented themselves at an ideal juncture in his development as a composer. The staging of the ballet ran into one obstacle after another. Since most of them arose from the subject matter of the libretto, it is worth relating the plot in some detail. The curtain rises on a backstreet room, barely furnished but with an open bed prominently displayed. On stage are three men and a girl, whom they urge to dance at the window in order to lure men in from the street. The first victim is an elderly drunk who is beaten and thrown out when his comic posturing turns to violence. He is followed by a timid youth, for whom the girl feels a tender attraction but he too is ejected when it is discovered that he has no money. At this point the Mandarin makes his entrance, a mysterious, inscrutable and awe-inspiring figure (Lengyel's original conception was a misshapen dwarf). As the girl, at once fascinated and repelled, starts again her erotic dance, he pursues her round the room, slowly at first, then with increasing frenzy. The three pimps emerge from hiding, set upon the Mandarin and suffocate him but, so unquenchable is his lust, he will not die. They stab him repeatedly and finally hang him from the ceiling, but only when the girl submits to him does the blood begin to flow from his wounds and, sated, he sinks and dies.

Although attitudes towards theatrical licence are more liberal now than in the 1920s, even so they were then not especially noted for prudery or austerity. The ballet was open to a number of interpretations — from the overwhelming strength of nature within man himself to the indomitable power of love over inhuman cruelty — but the Hungarian authorities could see no more than a seditious potion of criminal violence and flagrant sexuality. They vacillated and compromised interminably and eventually suggested that the affront to public morality might be mitigated by transferring the action to an anonymous, outdoor Asian setting. Thus it finally reached the Budapest stage, but, by then, twenty-five years had elapsed and Bartók was dead. However, it was given in Cologne, in 1926, where the scandal and outrage of the church and press was so violent that the mayor stepped in and banned the production after a single performance.

Bartók never returned to the theatre. He had no taste for the intrigues of theatrical life and was probably aware that his greatest gift was for instrumental music. This is not to discount the importance of a comparatively small number of vocal masterpieces, any more than to say the same of Beethoven belittles *Fidelio* or the *Missa Solemnis*. It was to this medium that he now returned, first with the *Eight Improvisations on Hungarian Peasant Songs* for piano, which represent his most extreme reworking of actual peasant material. There followed, in 1921 and 1922, two sonatas for violin and piano, neither of them calculated to win mass popularity, but which nevertheless contributed enormously to his standing in the international arena. They represent the extreme point of Bartók's experimentation with logical dissonance and this, together with certain melodic aspects, brings his music into closer proximity with the second Viennese school of Schoenberg than ever before or after. The galloping folk dance movements are, of course, pure

Bartók with his mother in 1925.
(Embassy of the Hungarian People's Republic)

61

Bartók but, if influences are to be discerned, then mention should also be made of the Polish composer Karol Szymanowski, whose works Bartók was studying eagerly at the time. Their composition coincided with a fortuitous re-meeting with the brilliant violinist Jelly Aranyi whom he had known in his student days. Her family had emigrated to London before the war, but she visited Budapest in 1921 and Bartók was thrilled by the fire and imagination of her playing. Both sonatas were dedicated to her although, oddly, she did not give the first performance of either. When she did collaborate with the composer in performances in Paris and London, their success was enormous. The Paris première of the first sonata was a particularly exciting occasion, and Jelly 'excelled herself', Bartók informed his mother. Henri Prunières, the French musicologist, gave a supper party after the concert which 'was attended by "half the leading composers of the world" — that is Ravel, Szymanowski, Stravinsky — as well as a few young notorious Frenchmen whom you would not know.'

The young 'notorieties' included Milhaud and Poulenc who both sent enthusiastic notes to Bartók about the sonata.

Folk music collecting was still moribund due to the continuing restrictions on travel, so activity in this field had to be confined to the organisation and classification of existing material. Bartók and Kodály organised voluntary seminars at the Academy to this end and work progressed steadily, although Antal Doráti recalled that most of the students attended through devotion to their teachers rather than any great enthusiasm for the painstaking chores involved.

Travel of a broader sort was on the increase again. Concert tours took him to England, Germany, Holland, France and Italy, as well as his beloved Transylvania. In the provinces he offered mixed programmes with Debussy and Scarlatti interspersed with the less demanding pieces by himself and Kodály, while the capitals were introduced to his toughest new works, such as the *Studies, op. 18* and the Violin Sonatas. Although the works composed between 1918 and 1923 are few, one can only marvel that he found time to compose at all. His public appearances in Budapest were largely confined to chamber music, but abroad, his reputation and the scope of his activity were growing year by year. English and French newspapers treated his appearances as events of major importance, and the enthusiasm of knowledgeable audiences was heartwarming. The Viennese *Musikblätter des Anbruch* devoted a whole issue to Bartók to mark his fortieth birthday, an event which passed unnoticed in Budapest.

Eventually, the Hungarian government no longer could hold aloof in the face of international acclaim. In 1923, on the occasion of the Jubilee of the union of the old towns of Buda and Pest, it

SI VIGADÓ   FŐVÁROSI VIGADÓ

Hétfőn, 1923. évi november hó 19-én este 7 órakor

UDA EGYESITÉSÉNEK 50-IK ÉVFORDULÓJA ALKALMÁBÓL

RENDKÍVÜLI

ARMÓNIAI DÍSZHANGVERSENY

Vezényel: MŰSOR:
DOHNÁNYI ERNŐ

Közreműködik:
ÉKELYHIDY FERENC
ALESTRINA KÓRUS
DOHNÁNYI ERNŐ

Poster for the concert in 1923 which signified the re-establishment of Bartók, Kodály and Dohnányi.

swallowed its pride and announced a Festival Concert featuring specially commissioned works by its three leading musicians, thus welcoming the black sheep back to the fold.

The programme read as follows,

Festival Overture	Dohnányi
Psalmus Hungaricus	Kodály
Dance Suite	Bartók

Even then, the rebels had something defiant to say to their chauvinist persecutors. Although Dohnányi produced a thoroughly respectable overture from unimpeachable sources, the other two made thinly veiled references in their scores to their recent experiences. Kodály's setting of a sixteenth century paraphrase of the fifty-fifth psalm contained words of an unmistakeable symbolic significance,

Better it were to dwell in the desert,
Better to hide me deep in the forest
Than live with wicked liars and traitors
Who will not suffer me to tell the truth.

while Bartók drew liberally on 'alien' Romanian and Arabic sources as well as Magyar idioms in his thrilling *Dance Suite*.

In one important aspect this exhilarating work marks the crossing of the last divide for the composer. Every theme in the suite is of Bartók's own invention and yet, never has the earthy source of his inspiration seemed more present. The assimiliation is complete, the mission in search of a 'truly national style' accomplished.

The *Dance Suite* was a more fitting and momentous contribution to this memorable evening in Hungarian music than the commissioning authorities can ever have imagined — or deserved.

Chapter Seven

The year 1923 was also a momentous one in Bartók's personal life. In the summer he and Marta were divorced and in August he married Ditta Pásztory, a twenty-one-year-old student who had entered his piano class at the Academy the previous year. Bartók may have found Marta's submissive nature oppressive (as has been suggested by one Hungarian researcher) or it may simply have been a case of irresistible attraction between teacher and pupil. The circumstances and background to this domestic upheaval have never been fully revealed and Bartók's nature would clearly have found any airing of his private life distasteful to a degree. In any event, it seems to have been Marta who urged him to take the irrevocable step and, as far as such a rift can be accomplished without undue pain and suffering, this was done. To judge from their letters, the main preoccupation of both was to allay the distress and anxiety of Paula Bartók and to consider the welfare of young Béla who 'understood the "specialness" of the situation.'

Otto Klemperer's recollection of a collaboration with Bartók some years later confirms that the break-up was achieved with a remarkable lack of rancour and bitterness.

He was a strange man — very reserved, very shy but very sympathetic. He had a new wife at the time. But the old one also came to the rehearsal, so he appeared with two wives!

The unnerving mixture of reserve and fanatical intensity made an indelible impact on many people who met Bartók. Their descriptions of his manner and personal appearance would suggest romantic hyperbole were it not for the unanimity of their impressions. Even those Academy students who had no direct contact with him felt the power of his presence as they passed in the corridors, and Antal Doráti's is typical of their reminiscences.

Bartók was rather small . . . very thin, pale, white-haired. (This is no mistake. Bartók had then at thirty-four, white-grey hair). He had thin lips, barely moving for a timid smile, and barely parting to allow softly-spoken words to be heard; a fine, straight nose and eyes! — there was never such a

Opposite Bartók and his second wife, Ditta Pásztory. (Embassy of the Hungarian People's Republic)

65

pair of eyes! Large, burning, piercing — his looks had something of a branding iron — they seemed to mark everybody on whom they fixed.

Besides the students and fellow musicians, there was a perceptive and outspoken critical faction, led by Aladár Tóth, which urged Bartók's compatriots to recognise and acclaim the emergence of a Hungarian composer of truly international stature. Foreign orchestras clamoured for the *Dance Suite* and it was presented by Pierre Monteux in Amsterdam, Frigyes (Fritz) Reiner in Cincinnati and Vaclav Talich in Prague within a year of the Budapest première, while, in 1925, it received over fifty performances in Germany alone.

By and large, though, the Budapest public did not really take him to its heart even at that time, and there was still considerable hostility towards him in reactionary quarters. However, the self-doubt and indecision that had afflicted him after earlier rebuffs was a thing of the past, and the fact that he produced only one work between 1923 and 1926 (*Village Scenes* — Slovak folk songs for female voice and piano) should not be attributed to dejection or loss of confidence but to the ever-increasing pressure of work in his other three fields — performing, teaching and research.

Although collecting tours were still not a practical proposition, work on the existing material was never forgotten. It was an enormous task, an unending one really, but this was more an attraction than a deterrent. Bartók regarded folk music as a pure source from whence he could renew his strength and replenish his imagination. A major landmark was the publication (Budapest, 1924) of an extensive treatise *Hungarian Peasant Music,* and the preparation of his collection of some three thousand Slovak folk songs was in progress intermittently from 1922 to 1928. Another collection, and one especially close to his heart, was of Romanian *Colinde* (Christmas Songs) and he had high hopes when keen interest was shown by a visiting representative of the Oxford University Press. However, he had not reckoned with the dilatory expansiveness of English academics and his pleasurable anticipation was succeeded by exasperated frustration at their leisurely ways. He eventually published a curtailed version at his own expense in Vienna but, since the whole saga dragged on over nine years, the eventual outcome can hardly be put down to unreasonable impatience on Bartók's part.

His literary activities were not confined to folk song and he contributed articles to various musical publications on subjects ranging from Schoenberg and Stravinsky to letters exchanged between Liszt and Mosonyi, not to mention all the entries on Hungarian music and musicians in *A Dictionary of Modern Music and Musicians* published in London in 1924.

Teaching remained something of a burden, but he was not a man to give of himself half-heartedly and his pupils remembered him with gratitude and affection.

I remember him as being rather soft-spoken and polite (Sir Georg Solti recalled), if he criticised anything, he always did so very gently ... I suppose my foremost feeling about Bartók was a sort of reverance of the kind one has for a priest or a pope. He was tremendously remote from us, and you never heard any gossip about him: he was absolutely pure, like a saint.

If he found it hard to reconcile himself to the administrative chores of teaching, there were incidental benefits which he cannot have foreseen. Many of his pupils were to be a source of help in the troubled years to come, and one of them, the conductor Frigyes (Fritz) Reiner, was already vigorously championing his works in America. The study of early keyboard music (Frescobaldi, Couperin and Marcello amongst them), which he initially undertook as a pedagogic exercise, provided valuable additions to his own repertoire as a pianist and, more significantly, added a new dimension to his next creative outburst.

Bartók's reputation as a pianist has perhaps been unduly overshadowed by his greatness as a composer. István Thomán maintained that, of contemporary pianists, Busoni and Bartók most closely approached the sovereignty of Liszt. One might incline towards indulgent scepticism at the judgement of a teacher on his favourite pupil, but Otto Klemperer's assessment is not to be lightly discounted.

He was a wonderful pianist and musician. The beauty of his tone, the energy and lightness of his playing were unforgettable. It was almost painfully beautiful. He played with great freedom, that was what was so wonderful.

Others remarked on the lucidity and integrity of his interpretations, but this evidently did not preclude the occasional eruption of volcanic energy from his slight frame, as a startled Olin Downes reported,

... he showed a born instinct for the keyboard with poetry of conception and at times a fury of virtuosity and élan astonishing in a man of his modesty and unostentation.

Concert tours in several European countries were now annual events and, although he grudged the time involved, he enjoyed the liberating effects of travel which brought escape from the claustrophobic pressures of Budapest. If official circles at home showed scant appreciation of his worth, the neighbouring Romanians left him in no doubt of the warmth of their admiration, and he was given a tremendous reception on a return visit in October, 1923. An extensive tour of the provinces culminated in a piano recital in Bucharest, and a chamber music concert the following day (organised by the Association of Romanian Composers) brought together the leading musicians of the two countries in a performance of the *Second Violin Sonata* with George Enescu and the composer. The Romanian government crowned this triumphant occasion by bestowing on Bartók an official accolade, the Bene Merenti Order (1st Class).

This shameless fraternisation with the erstwhile enemy was inevitably not to the liking of the right wingers in Budapest and they wasted no time in renewing their wearisome sniping. Despite Bartók's scathing comments on the ineptitudes of the Kun administration, he was regarded as a communist by the hard-liners and repeatedly attacked for his association with left-wing emigrés. There were even threats of violence when plans were announced to revive the two Balázs stage works. In response to persistent pressure, the Ministry of Culture initiated proceedings against Bartók for playing in the still disputed Transylvanian region, now officially Romanian territory. The charge was soon dropped, but Bartók must have derived quiet amusement at the Romanian government's retaliatory gesture in refusing an entry permit to Jenö Hubay who had planned to give some concerts in the country in 1924.

By now, Bartók was fairly phlegmatic about this sort of behaviour and, if he felt a twinge of pique as his major works were consistently overlooked when it came to the allocation of national awards and prizes, he had only to look beyond the Hungarian border to be reassured of his standing. He had been enlisted by the energetic English scholar, Edward J. Dent, into the activities of the newly-formed International Society for Contemporary Music, and, from now on, his works were a regular feature of the society's festival promotions. The Prague newspaper *Bohemia* in a report of a performance of the *Dance Suite* at the 1925 Festival showed that his music was not only admired by foreign musicians, but also increasingly understood.

Bartók gives us no more syncopated pieces in the *Czardas* manner nor over-sentimentalised tunes; he has gone back to the original sources of Hungarian folk song and dance, and has recreated them in a manner of his own. A kind of music of barbaric power in its rhythms and ebullient temperament, that carries itself along with urgent excitement has emerged. . . . No work by any of the other foreign composers was given such a tumultuous reception, and Bartók had to take call after call.

To be singled out from composers of the calibre of Stravinsky, Janáček, Milhaud, Busoni and Vaughan Williams must have warmed even Bartók's reticent heart, but perhaps not so radiantly as a repetition of this brilliant performance (by the Czech Philharmonic Orchestra under Vaclav Talich) in Budapest later in the year which was encored in its entirety. This popular success at home did something to alleviate his underlying sadness that he, of all people, should have been pilloried for 'un-Hungarian activities'. Just a year earlier, in November, 1924, he had ruefully observed to a foreign journalist,

There may come a time when I shall be recognised as a Hungarian composer. Though perhaps by that time I shall no longer be alive.

As a pianist, Bartók was necessarily presenting a somewhat out-of-date image of himself. His last piano work had been the *Improvisations* of 1920, so his programmes could give no hint of the enormous strides made in the *Dance Suite* and the two *Violin Sonatas*. Consequently, when he took up his pen again in 1926, he concerned himself almost exclusively with his own instrument and, after a summer of furious creative work, his repertoire was enriched by the *Piano Sonata*, the suite *Out of Doors*, the *Nine Little Piano Pieces* and his *First Piano Concerto* which, taken as a group, admirably exemplified his current position, encompassing characteristics of both his recent instrumental works and those which were shortly to follow.

The *Nine Little Piano Pieces* bear witness to his studies of the early keyboard composers, and introduce a new contrapuntal ingenuity which was to be an integral feature of his music from now on. They have been cited, too, as an excursion into the 'neo-classicism' then in vogue. The retreat from romanticism took many forms and the objectivity of the baroque masters seemed to many composers an ideal worth recapturing. Poulenc, Hindemith and, especially, Stravinsky went along this road at various times, and so too did Debussy and Ravel, though without the same self-conscious ostentation. Bartók certainly knew Stravinsky's early 'neo-classical' works, but was repelled by his aesthetic argument that music is incapable of expressing anything other than itself.

'Bach also expressed something — some moments of life,' said Bartók, and these pieces (though hardly to be counted among his greatest) conspicuously avoid the element of artifice and pastiche that has so rapidly dated so many works of the school.

Nevertheless, the polyphonic experience added a further rich dimension to his language, and his ability to absorb and profit from fresh ideas and influences without compromising his individuality is a measure of his ability to transmute life's experience into art.

The harsh, brutal drive of Bartók's piano music had ruffled the sensibilities of conservative souls ever since he had unleashed the *Allegro Barbaro* on the world in 1911. In 1915, the critic of the learned *Musical Quarterly* had likened his pieces to

Unmeaning bunches of notes apparently representing the composer promenading the keyboard in his boots,

and he wrote himself into the history of philistinism by concluding

Some can be played better with the elbows, others with the flat of the hand. None require fingers to perform nor ears to listen to.

'Ugly and incoherent,' grumbled *The Sunday Times*, and the name Bartók came to symbolise everything that the bewildered layman associated with 'modern music' in much the same way as Picasso symbolised 'modern art'. The *Piano Sonata* must have confirmed the uneasy expectations of traditionalists, just as it thrilled the more adventurous. Although its ebullient rhythmic vitality has much in common with the *Dance Suite*, the monochrome nature of the instrument and Bartók's unequivocally percussive treatment of it underlines the atavistic barbarism of the peasant rhythms and the starkness of the melodies. The slow movement, traditionally the expressive core of a sonata, begins with a single note struck twenty times without nuance and with the barest rhythmic inflection, before resolving downwards to complete the melodic statement, and this is accompanied by colourless, impassive dissonances in the left hand. Some of the pianistic devices can be traced back to Liszt and it is possible to point to parallels with Beethoven in the adaptation of traditional forms to accommodate specific threads of argument, but these are superficial comparisons when viewed alongside the boldness and sheer originality of the conception which make the sonata a major landmark in piano literature. These observations apply to many aspects of the *First Piano Concerto* which features the same percussive piano writing and primitive thematic material. Bartók was sorely in need of a new vehicle for his appearances with orchestra. He had hitherto been relying on the *Rhapsody No. 1* which was no longer representative, although he always retained a special affection for it partly, no doubt, on account of its rejection at the Rubinstein competition. The significance of a fully-fledged concerto was quickly acknowledged and the first performance (in Frankfurt under Furtwängler) was followed by others with such important conductors as Erich Kleiber and Pierre Monteux.

The central movement of the *Out of Doors* suite, *Night Music* (dedicated to Ditta), introduces us to a further uniquely Bartókian

Bartók on holiday in
Switzerland during the thirties.

sound-world, a magical evocation of the sounds and atmosphere of nature at night; not the langourous nocturnal dreams of Chopin, still less the vapid effusions of the countless nineteenth century piano pieces entitled 'At the Brook' or 'Forest Murmurs'. Nor has Bartók's vision much in common with the romantic, pantheistic view of Beethoven's *Pastoral Symphony* or Smetana's *Ma Vlast*. His natural world is alive with the chirping and twittering of insects, the eerie rustle of twigs and undergrowth, the sudden screech of a frightened bird.

These sounds evoke the reality of a night beyond the realm of earth, Bartók's own night (wrote the critic Aladár Tóth after the first performance). This is one of the most marvellous masterpieces to capture the poetry of nature in Hungary.

Bartók's absorbing interest in the natural world was nothing new. Back in 1907, had he not proclaimed to Stefi Geyer, 'if I ever crossed myself it would be in the name of Nature, Art and Science'? Folk music itself he regarded as a natural phenomenon and in the course of his explorations he had amassed a sizeable supplementary collection of insects, moths and shells and a thorough knowledge of natural history to go with it. In his last years in America, onlookers were startled at the sight of a frail old man prodding at cowdung with his stick and peering intently at the teeming life within.

71

Bartók—as seen by a New York
cartoonist.

It was at this time that Bartók paid his first visit to the land that
was to be his final resting place. An extensive concert tour of the
USA was arranged for December, 1927 and January, 1928. His first
impressions were mixed. Though bewildered by 'the maddening
hubbub everywhere,' he admired the exuberant vitality of the
people but found the unquestioned supremacy of commercialism
depressing. The schedule was an exceptionally arduous one, not
only in the sheer number of engagements but also the vastness of
distances travelled. Orchestral performances, chamber music and
solo recitals jostled with one another in bewildering profusion. An
additional strain was the half-hour lecture with which he prefaced
his solo recitals, which taxed his command of English to the utmost.
Nonetheless, he welcomed the opportunity to spread a little
propaganda for Hungarian music and to clear up a few misconcep-
tions about his own work.

There was little time to indulge his insatiable traveller's
curiosity, but he did visit a Chinese theatre in San Francisco ('I was
the only white man present except for the doorman') and also had
his first taste of real jazz. Contrary to some reports, he did not
disapprove.

72

In the past few days, I have heard real Negro jazz in a speakeasy in Chicago. This was really good. They played from a score but many times they improvised and this was fascinating.

But he did make it clear where his allegiance lay,

We have no need for jazz. We have beautiful folk music of our own and it is superfluous to fling ourselves into the arms of jazz.

By the end of January, the wear and tear of incessant travelling and waiting listlessly in stations and overheated hotel rooms had taken its toll of his frail constitution and he was more than ready to return home, and on March 6th he was on his way.

Two other masterpieces adorn this richly productive period. Bartók's string quartets, like Beethoven's, present a kind of résumé of his achievement, crystallising the stages in the development of his mature style with a conciseness that makes the individual works stand out as peaks in a panoramic view of his achievement.

The *Third String Quartet* of 1927 is the shortest but perhaps the hardest to assimilate of the series, and thus sums up what is sometimes described as Bartók's 'expressionist' period, which encompasses *The Miraculous Mandarin*, the two violin sonatas and certain aspects of the piano music of 1926. The harmonic idiom is harsh and grating, the structural organisation intensely compressed and the percussive chordal conclusion rivals the piano music in its barbaric violence. Bartók submitted this work for a competition organised by the Musical Trust Fund of Philadelphia and, to his surprise and delight, he and Alfredo Casella shared the first prize of six thousand dollars, which caused great commotion at home.

You can hardly imagine what sensation this created in Budapest. Six thousand dollars! I told everybody from the outset that it just couldn't be as much as that — but all to no effect; it is by now common knowledge that I won 6,000.

Even so, his share of three thousand dollars was a wonderful tonic and his first major financial reward. By a curious anomaly, the forgotten composer H. Waldo Warner, who was awarded joint second prize and outright third, won more in actual cash than the two first prize winners.

The *Fourth String Quartet* followed about a year later, after Bartók's return from the States. It shows the same rigorous logic as its predecessor, but the design is expanded to five movements. Overall structure becomes an increasingly dominant consideration from this point, and the 'arch' form is a prototype for several later works. In simple terms, this 'arch' can best be described as a

73

Bartók with the violinists Zoltan
Székely . . .

palindrome, the outer movements being closely related, the second and fourth likewise, with the central slow movement forming the cornerstone. This increasing preoccupation with architectural design should not in the least imply a dilution or supression of expressive intensity. The 'cello's passionate Magyar lament in the slow movement, the magical sounds of the night, the scurrying whirlwind *Prestissimo* could hardly be more direct in their emotional impact.

The string quartets have been analysed inside out by subsequent generations of musicologists but, although Bartók relished the intellectual grappling that their researches have unearthed, he was not insensitive to practical considerations, and his friendlier face is nowhere more disarmingly revealed than in the two virtuoso *Rhapsodies* he composed for the violinists József Szigeti and Zoltán Székely during this period. His was not a facile talent, but, through unflinching perseverance and artistic integrity, he had now acquired the complete mastery to give unfettered expression to his genius no matter what external factors were to govern his choice of forces or medium.

. . . and József Szigeti,
dedicatees of the two
Rhapsodies.

Chapter Eight

The complete assurance with which he now approached his work enabled Bartók to free himself from any self-protective limitations. Although he never once throughout his career stooped to anything which could be remotely described as commercialism, he was able to capitalise to a limited extent on his success. People now came to *him* with pleas and commissions for new works and he was able to adapt to their requirements. He orchestrated the piano *Sonatina* (under the title *Transylvanian Dances*) and some of the *Fifteen Hungarian Peasant Songs* which he freely admitted was

Bartók in March 1927.

now an orchestral suite which I put together for the money. This is the sort of thing that will be performed because the music is pleasing, it is not very difficult to play and it is by a 'known' composer.

In the two *Rhapsodies* he also overcame his earlier aversion to urban popular music, making use of nineteenth century 'verbunkos' elements for the first time. He had made his point that this sort of thing did not represent the true basis of Hungarian folk music, and he was now able to see it as part and parcel of his country's musical culture. He emerged from his ivory tower secure in the knowledge that his own musical personality was fully formed and incorruptible.

After his travels in Europe and the United States, there was but one field left to conquer, and that was put in hand for the very end of 1929 and the first half of January, 1930. There was naturally considerable antagonism at government level between the Soviet Union and Horthy's Hungary, but tenuous cultural links had been maintained. There was much musicological nonsense written in Soviet journals about 'bourgeois heritage' and 'leftism' in the arts, but the dictates of 'socialist realism' had not yet taken its stranglehold on the development and dissemination of modern ideas and, in Moscow and Leningrad at least, there was a lively avant-garde.

Bartok's tour of the USSR began in Kharkov and thence to Odessa and Leningrad. Political considerations at once took a backseat to his perennial passion,

The folklore collections I saw, particularly those in Petersburg, were impressive and most valuable,

and his comments on the economic situation were restricted to practical observations,

There are practically no good pianos at all; the old ones are worn out and cannot be repaired because all the materials have to be imported.

The friendly warmth of the people was very appealing and Bartók was good humoured and indulgent about the sometimes chaotic disorganisation of his schedule. Concerts had to be cancelled because insufficient time had been allowed for travelling between venues, and it was by no means certain which trains would run or how long they would take to reach their destination.

But apart from this, (he wrote to Ditta), they are very charming people, and they have loaded me with scores and folk song publications (I shall have plenty to drag home with me). The audience also proved to be very enthusiastic at the end of the concert; they shouted bis! bis! (encore! encore!), and there were 3 encores. After the concert we went to a 'lordly' mansion, now owned by the Ukrainian People's Commissariat, where a banquet was held to seal the Hungaro-Ukrainian friendship.

It was refreshing to find that audiences were genuinely 'of the people' and not restricted to an élite section of society as was often the case in European and American halls. And everywhere their enthusiasm was heartwarming and spontaneous.

The whole tour lasted barely three weeks, so there was little time for idle tourism, but he found plenty of incidental delights to add to his store of traveller's memories.

Moscow looks just as one knows it from pictures: the roofs loaded with snow, so that they seem ready to cave in, and little one-horse sledges tinkling everywhere . . . Maupassant is right when he says that one ought to come here in the middle of winter (just as one ought to go to Africa in the height of summer); it is then that the country is at its most characteristic.

Once again, he arrived home feeling ill and exhausted, but there was scarcely time to recuperate before he was off on his travels again — this time to Switzerland where he appeared in two concerts of his own music at the end of January. It would be irksome to record all of his concert appearances in Europe, as they were now a routine feature of his existence, but this visit to Basle and Zurich (under the *aegis* of the ISCM) was significant for a number of reasons. In the first place, it marked a reunion with Stefi Geyer (now living with her husband in Zurich) who appeared with Bartók along with the singer Ilona Durigo, and it was also the occasion of

Bartók with the composer Conrad Beck and Paul Sacher, the conductor who secured the commissions for some of Bartók's greatest works of the 1930s.
(Embassy of the Hungarian People's Republic)

The Congress of Arab Music.
Paul Hindemith and his wife
are on the left.

The Congress of Arab Music.
Paul Hindemith and his wife
are on the left.

his first meeting with Mrs Müller-Widman of Basle, an admirer who was to become a close and devoted friend in time of need. Paul Sacher, the energetic young conductor of the Basle Chamber Orchestra, came into Bartók's life at this point too. Sacher was one of the great champions of twentieth century music, enlarging the repertoire of the chamber orchestra with commissions from several major composers, and it is to his friendship and influence that we owe three of Bartók's greatest masterpieces of the late 1930's, the *Music for Strings, Percussion and Celesta*, the *Sonata for Two Pianos and Percussion* and the *Divertimento* for string orchestra. In a tribute delivered shortly after Bartók's death, he presented a vivid portrait of the composer.

Whoever met Bartók, thinking of the rhythmic strength of his work, was surprised by his slight, delicate figure. He had the outward appearance of a fine-nerved scholar. Possessed of fanatical will and pitiless severity, and propelled by an ardent spirit, he affected inaccessibility and was reservedly polite. His being breathed light and brightness; his eyes burned with a noble fire. In the flash of his searching glance no falseness or obscurity could endure. If in a performance an especially hazardous and refractory passage came off well, he laughed in boyish glee; and when he was pleased with the successful solution of a problem, he actually beamed.

It was not just his music that took him abroad, but also his reputation as a musicologist. Such ventures were not always rewarding; he was happiest working in the field or in his study, and the world of congresses, seminars and academic one-upmanship was not his natural milieu. Once such event was the congress of Geneva in 1931, organised by the League of Nations Committee for International Co-operation. As a social occasion it had its attractions and he enjoyed the company of such eminent men of letters as Thomas

78

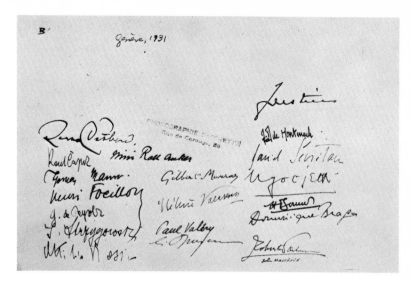

Mann and Paul Valéry, but the attendant official functions were not so palatable. A dinner given by the Hungarian Minister came in for acid comment in a long letter to Paula Bartók.

There were 5 or 6 wine glasses at each place of expensive Venetian glass, with dolphin shaped stems. Before lunch, delicious cocktails (brandy), at the end of the meal — Tokay (this, of course, is as it should be at the Hungarian Minister's). Nevertheless the lunch wasn't pleasant; what with the horrid screeching of Mrs X (the Minister's American wife) and these smooth and cunning diplomats — there's no getting away from it, they are an artificial crowd, quite different from artists.

The proceedings of the congress soon got bogged down in protocol, sub-committees and points of order, but Bartók refused to be disheartened, and he shows an unsuspected gift for humorous irony as he describes his own contribution. As the only musician present, he was urged to table a proposal:

I explained that I could only propose things that would cost a lot of money; they answered that it did not matter. So far so good; so I went ahead that evening and drafted something (about gramophone records) . . . A sub-committee was formed, we drafted a resolution, which was of course far different from the original and of no use, but it needed no money.

This was his first experience of the subtle cut and thrust of academic backbiting, and he looked on with fascinated amazement.

It is very amusing to see one speaker's reactions to another. They all begin by saying that they heard the proposal made by the previous speaker with the greatest pleasure and enjoyment, that the ideas were excellent, but that this wasn't quite accurate, and needed slight changes before being put into practice, or that something else was incorrect — in the end it turned out

79

that nothing said by the previous speaker was any good at all. However, politeness is the prime consideration. One thing you can be quite sure about, and that is that there will never be any violence on this Comité.

This sort of thing he could take lightly and with an engaging touch of self-mockery — as he did the farcical episode of a summer school at Mondsee where hardly any of the pupils turned up — but there were disquieting political developments on which his conscience forbade him to keep silent. He had been outspokenly critical of the anti-semitic tendencies of the Horthy government from the start, as we have seen, and as fascism crept into the fabric of Italian and German life his anxiety and disapproval demanded public expression. When, in 1931, Arturo Toscanini was beaten up and virtually drummed out of Italy by fascists for refusing to conduct the *Giovinezza* (fascist march), Bartók drafted a resolution to the ISCM urging the society to take immediate action at the forthcoming session in Oxford to counteract the growing state interference with artistic freedom and to formulate proposals 'for the protection of the integrity and autonomy of the arts.'

He was, of course, far from happy with the political situation in Hungary itself. The Horthy régime was now solidly entrenched and, despite its nationalistic posturing, did little to improve the lot of the common people. Horthy himself relied heavily on the support of the old ruling classes and his two henchmen, Count István Bethlen and General Gyula Gömbös were, respectively, a died in the wool aristocrat and an out and out careerist. Little if anything was done to alleviate the appalling poverty amongst the peasantry, and the occasional outbursts of left-wing intellectuals failed to arouse a genuine popular response. The traditional restrictive measures of authoritarian régimes — for instance, the banning of trade unionism in key areas such as agriculture and public services — kept a tight rein on the status quo, and it seemed to some democrats that the Hapsburg court had simply transferred from Vienna to Budapest. Official historians seemed to be advocating a return to feudalism, and these reactionary forces were unrelenting in their attempts to belittle the work of Bartók and Kodály. One such writer who particularly infuriated Bartók was the critic and composer Emil Haraszti, who derided Kodály's 'faithful folklore and artistic primitivism,' at the same time eulogising the gypsy musician 'whose like as an artist cannot be found anywhere in the world.'

In 1930, the Romanian folklorist and scholar, Octavian Beu, prepared a radio programme on Bartók and submitted his text for the composer's approval. Bartók's reply has been much quoted, and rightly so, for it contains a serious and valuable attempt at self-assessment, as well as some amusing side-swiping at Haraszti.

I must inform you that Haraszti is a stupid and, in addition, a malicious man who, moreover, understands as much of music as a hen does of the ABC.

Elsewhere in this revealing document, Bartók is at pains to clarify the relative importance of Hungarian, Romanian and Slovak folk music in his own work, and at the same time reveals a deep humanitarian concern which is a far cry from the narrow nationalistic road which he started out along thirty years before.

My creative work, just because it arises from three sources (Hungarian, Romanian, Slovakian), might be regarded as the very embodiment of the very concept of integration so much emphasised in Hungary today. Of course, I do not write this for you to make it public; you will yourself beware of doing so, for such ideas are not for the Romanian press. I only mention it as a possible point of view which I encountered about ten years ago, when I was attacked in the most violent manner as a musical Scotus Viator. My own idea, however — of which I have been fully conscious since I found myself as a composer — is the brotherhood of peoples, brotherhood in spite of wars and conflicts. I try — to the best of my ability — to serve this idea in my music; therefore I don't reject any influence, be it Slovakian, Romanian, Arabic or from any other source. The source must only be clean, fresh and healthy! Owing to my — let us say — geographical position, it is the Hungarian source that is nearest to me, and therefore the Hungarian influence is the strongest. Whether my style — notwithstanding its various sources — has a Hungarian character or not (and that is the point) — is for others to judge, not for me. For my own part, I certainly feel that it has. For character and milieu must somehow harmonise with each other.

Bartok's fastidious conscience could be positively obstructive at times. In January, 1931, shortly before his fiftieth birthday, he received a letter from a Mr Tamasiu inviting him to attend the festivities associated with the unveiling of a plaque in his honour at Nagyszentmiklós, his birthplace (now in Romania and renamed Sinnicolaul Mare). Bartók replied coldly that he was not fond of ceremonies, nor did like the idea of 'squeezing money out of people' for such a project. On receiving assurances that the cost was trifling and the money already collected, he yielded slightly but imposed a condition that the plaque be inscribed in Hungarian as well as Romanian. The deterioration in relations between Hungary and her neighbours meant that Bartók's friends in Czechoslovakia and Romania had to fight to protect him from attacks by their own nationalist cliques. In any event, it all came to nothing and a suitable memorial was not erected until 1951.

An appetite for public acclaim was never a driving force in Bartók's life and by this time he was so disillusioned with political and cultural conditions in Budapest that he had again virtually

retired from public life there. All his major works were premièred abroad, and for six years he made only occasional appearances as a pianist in the capital, and then only to play music by other composers or to renew collaborations with old friends such as Dohńanyi or Imre Waldbauer. Plans had been afoot again to revive the stage works and Béla Balázs, from exile, waived his rights to royalties and public billing in the hope that this might ease their path, but to no avail. Yet another attempt to get *The Miraculous Mandarin* onto the stage at last met with a similar fate.

The French recognised Bartók's fiftieth birthday by making him 'Chevalier de la legion d'honneur', and the Hungarian authorities made a belated attempt to match this by awarding him the Corvin Wreath. Bartók did not attend the ceremony, and his feelings were probably accurately divined in a moving tribute by Aládár Tóth in the paper *Pesti Naplo*:

It is not for us to hasten with gifts to an artist when we made no haste to accept the gifts he had to offer; it is not for us to disturb the privacy of an artist whom we ourselves would have none of. We have no right to feel proud of an artist who was born among us and lived for us, but whom we did not accept as one of ourselves. The time is not ripe for a Bartók celebration in Hungary. First we must work for this genius, then we can honour him.

Indeed, Bartók's depression was deepening. Wherever he looked, he saw evil poisoning the everyday lives of ordinary people. He was one of the first to set his face implacably against Nazism, and from 1933 he never played in Germany again. Likewise, Franco's victory in the Spanish civil war signified the end of his association with that country with all its happy memories of his early concert tours. He

82

fostered his connections in England, Belgium, France, Holland and Switzerland but, from this time, he held little hope for the future of Europe.

Happily for subsequent generations, his zest for composition was undiminished. In 1932, he moved with Ditta and their young son Peter into a comfortable house on the Csalan-ut, their last home in Hungary, where he was able to work in peace in his studio on the second floor, and it was here that a new series of major works was born. This new wave had begun two years earlier with the great *Cantata Profana* for two soloists, full choir and orchestra, to his own text based upon a Romanian folk ballad which expresses something of his hopes and dreams for the destiny of man. There is good reason to believe that Bartók had in mind a triptych of cantatas, the other two to be based on Hungarian and Slovak folklore — thus serving the ideal of the brotherhood of nations outlined in his letter to Octavian Beu. The idea never came to fruition, so the *Cantata*

Bartók's shorthand 'aide-memoire' for the *Second Piano Concerto*.

Profana stands as a unique edifice in Bartók's oeuvre; although the ballad style shows some affinity with *Duke Bluebeard's Castle* and the nature imagery some echoes of *The Wooden Prince*, its style is unlike either and the forces employed are dissimilar to those in any other of his works. The cantata is shot through with Bartók's most earthy melody, enriched by strong, woody colouring and an amazing contrapuntal fecundity (Kódaly stated that Bartók was studying Palestrina's choral style at the time). The ballad tells of an old man whose nine sons go hunting in wild country. They come to a mysterious bridge and, on crossing it, are turned into stags. The old man begs them to return, but they choose to remain in their transformed state, united with nature. The message is unmistakable; that sacrifice must be made if man is to find his way back to a pure way of life — in Bartók's words, 'to drink only from the clear spring.'

Then there is the magnificent *Second Piano Concerto*, a brilliant virtuoso vehicle for the soloist and the work of a virtuoso composer too, revelling in his mastery of every facet of his craft, juggling with all manner of contrapuntal devices with effortless legerdemain and bewitching his audience with the bright, clean 'baroque' flavour of the first movement, the still, soulful Adagio with its whirring 'night music' intermezzo and the barbaric splendour of the finale. Bartók spoke disarmingly of the 'light' and 'popular' character of the themes in this Titan among piano concertos. The first performance in Frankfurt was also Bartók's last appearance in Germany. Even for this brilliant vehicle, he was not to be persuaded to emerge from his withdrawal from the Budapest stage and the Hungarian première was entrusted to Lajos (Louis) Kentner.

Between 1930 and 1935 Bartók wrote an unusual amount of vocal music, and besides the cantata, mention should also be made of the *Twenty Hungarian Folk Songs* with piano accompaniment and, for chorus, the *Four Hungarian Folk Songs* and the *Six Székely Songs*. Young musicians benefited during this period from the *44 Duos* for two violins and the eight volumes of choruses for school choirs (with and without orchestra).

Finally, the great series of string quartets received fresh impetus in the shape of a commission from the Elizabeth Sprague Coolidge Foundation. This, the *Fifth Quartet*, which continues the five movement format established in the fourth, was composed at white heat in exactly one month at the end of the summer of 1934 and the first performance was given in Washington by the Kolisch Quartet the following April.

An unexpected blessing came to ease the tribulations of the aging composer. In September, 1934, he was relieved of his teaching duties at the Academy and offered a long coveted research post by the Hungarian Academy of Sciences, of which he became a member in May, 1935.

Chapter Nine

This change in Bartók's routine did not entail any lessening of his workload; far from it. He had been pressing for an officially sponsored collection of Hungarian folk tunes since 1913, and had frequently castigated the government for allowing neighbouring countries to steal a march on them by publishing their own collections. There was a mass of work to be done and, although his dream did not come to fruition until after his death (when the Hungarian Academy of Sciences published the first of a series of volumes in 1951), much of the source work was the result of Bartók's steadfast endeavour. In all, he sorted and categorised some 13,000 Hungarian melodies, in addition to his ancillary work on folk music of other nations which continued at the same time. There were inevitable but infuriating obstacles to overcome, now that the whole business had become so entangled with the nationalist squabbles of Eastern Europe. Bartók, although he could not ignore the problem, tried to stand aloof from all political considerations and he made his attitude plain in a letter to the Croatian folklorist, Vinko Zganec.

Please believe me when I say that in my studies I have not been, and never shall be, guided by any chauvinistic bias; my sole aim is to search for the truth and to conduct my search with as much impartiality as is humanly possible. As the clearest proof of this I can point to my explicit statement in this booklet (of his radio talks) that approximately 38 per cent of the Hungarian material is of foreign, chiefly Slovak, origin, while only about 20 per cent of the Slovak material is of Hungarian origin (all this, of course, on the basis of the material collected so far; additional collecting might change the picture).

The reality of political obstructionism was firmly brought home to him when the booklet was returned by the Yugoslav customs marked 'Forbidden Material', and the elusive nature of his scientific objectives is indicated by the proviso in parentheses. Time and time again he had to revise his conclusions as new probabilities and inter-relationships emerged from his studies of Bulgarian, Slovak, Ruthenian, Serbo Croatian and other source material. Some understanding of the problem involved can be gathered from his important essay 'The Folk Music of Hungary

Transcribing recordings of folk music.

and the Neighbouring Peoples' (1934). Information gathered from his visit to the Congress for Arab Music in Cairo, in 1932, and to Turkey, in 1936, further complicated the picture. At times, he inclined to the belief that all the world's folk music would eventually be traced back to a handful of simple scales.

Some musicians, notably Stravinsky, have expressed regret that a composer of Bartók's genius should have expended so much time and energy on the pursuit of folk music, but, in truth, Bartók the composer and Bartók the folklorist are so inextricably intertwined that there is good reason to suppose that the one could not have existed without the other. His own view is cogently expressed in two further essays on 'Why and How Do We Collect Folk Music?' (1936) and 'The Influence of Peasant Music on Modern Music' (1931). The latter piece pinpoints Bartók's own position succinctly, even if the generality of the title elicits some special pleading when applied to other composers.

At the beginning of the twentieth century there was a turning point in the history of modern music.

The excesses of the Romanticists began to be unbearable for many. There were many composers who felt: 'this road does not lead us anywhere; there is no solution but a complete break with the nineteenth century.'

Invaluable help was given to this change (or rather let us call it rejuvenation) by a kind of peasant music unknown till then . . . It is the ideal starting point for a musical renaissance, and a composer in search of new ways cannot find a better master. What is the best way for a composer to reap the full benefits of his studies in peasant music? It is to assimilate the idiom of peasant music so completely that he is able to forget all about it and use it as his mother tongue.

From the earliest days of his discovery, Bartók never questioned the validity of this course. For him, it was both the alchemy of his creative genius and an absorbing passion in its own right, and never did he begrudge the hours of toil involved. Letters had to be written to colleagues in other countries and the interplay of scientific data was painstakingly recorded and correlated with his own material.

Inevitably, he ran into chauvinistic criticism from time to time but he accepted it, as a rule, as an irritating concomitant to his work. Nevertheless, it pained him that he should be the subject of attacks from xenophobes in Romania, where he had so recently been the object of adulation. Smears against him were initiated by various obscure informants (a bank manager from Brassó seems to have started it all) which resulted in his being banned from entering the country for a while, but the petty absurdity of the whole affair can best be seen from the final episode in 1937. Bartók had been

In the field—with members of the nomadic Kumarli tribe.

87

taunted beyond endurance by an article by Coriolan Petranu, a teacher at Cluj university, which accused him of distorting his information in the interests of 'Hungarian revisionism'. He published a blistering retort refuting the charges one by one, and this comment (on one of Petranu's more purple passages) conveys something of the acid contempt of Bartók's reply.

> We must acknowledge that these lines could have embellished any novel written a century ago; it is nevertheless impossible for us, although we are most willing, to detect in them any scientific value.

And what was the subject of this acrimonious exchange? The very same article on 'The Romanian Folk Music Dialect of Hunyad', written way back in 1915, over which Bartók had already weathered the insults of his own countrymen for its alleged anti-Hungarianism.

His compatriots did not leave him in peace now either. Under the Horthy government there had arisen an influential body of reactionary Catholic intellectuals who were strongly represented in the Ministry of Education, and it was from this quarter that the next attack came. It seemed to the adherents of this group that official condemnation of the progressive views of Bartòk and Kodály was weakening, and it is certainly true that there was a gradual, if belated, shift in the establishment press towards recognition of the country's two outstanding composers. Kodály had been an energetic advocate of educational reform at the most fundamental level ever since his days on the ill-fated Music Committee of 1919, and it is to his unflagging zeal in this direction that Hungary owes its lively and widely admired musical education system today. Bartók, though less active in this field, wholeheartedly supported Kodály's aims, and the performance of his children's choruses gave him especial delight.

> I shall never forget this impression of the freshness and gaiety of the little ones' voices. There is something in the natural way these children from the suburban schools produce their voices that reminds me of the unspoilt sound of peasant singing.

The clerical press did not share his enthusiasm. Their attack was partly political, but at least equally philistine in motivation. The campaign began in 1937, with an unsigned editorial in *Magyar Kultúra*, a paper owned by a wealthy Jesuit preacher, Béla Bangha. The article deplored the increasing official support for the work of the two composers and took the view that this progressive nonsense, like Ady's poetry, reflected the spirit of 'a bleak and destructive soul' and that its consumption should be confined to adults only. Its official encouragement in schools and youth choirs, it continued, could only lead to the pollution of the ideals of the young, and its use in church, the writer felt, was little short of blasphemous (Kodály's exciting motet 'Jesus and the Traders' had recently caused quite a stir).

The progressive intelligentsia reached for their pens and a lively battle of ink ensued. It was all something of a storm in a teacup and Bartók, on this occasion, was not to be drawn.

When a person is in the public eye, anything can be said about him . . . What is destructive about my music? Even the writer of the article could not say. I cannot try to improve my work since I do not know what they are complaining about. I consider the whole thing beneath my attention.

However, the passion which the episode aroused does indicate the predominance of reactionary aesthetics in influential circles which militated against Bartók throughout his career. The learned Kisfaludy Society had already furnished evidence of this when they decided to award him their prestigious Greguss Medal in 1936. This was a decidedly back-handed compliment, for the society made it clear that the award was not in respect of any of the internationally acclaimed masterpieces of the preceding ten years, but specifically for the immature, but comparatively euphonious *Suite no. 1* for orchestra of 1905. Bartók spat the trinket out in disgust, and his letter of rejection to the society is worth reproducing *in toto*.

Gentlemen:
I have read in today's papers that the Kisfaludy Society has awarded to me this year the Greguss Medal for my Suite for Orchestra No. 1 (Op. 3). I would like to add the following remarks to that:
1. The Society's statement of motivation is erroneous in regard to the first complete Hungarian performance of this work: it was performed in its entirety not in November, 1929 but, thank God, in 1909 by Jenö Hubay and later by Antal Fleischer on November 29, 1920. I say 'thank God' because it would be peculiar if in Hungary twenty-four years had passed before the first complete performance of a work composed in 1905 and of such excellence that it is deserving of the Greguss Medal.
2. Even if this statement of motivation is true — just as it is untrue — there would be something amiss in the award. I do very much like this work of mine; it is really an outstanding achievement for a young man twenty-four years of age. But in the period of 1929-1934 much better and more mature works were presented in Hungary, for instance, *The Spinning Room* or *Dances of Galanta* (both by Z. Kódaly).
3. Though unbidden I give friendly advice: it is urgent that you appoint another adviser in this matter. How can someone judge the value of a work, who is unable to decide — on account of external chronological conditions — which compositions are to be considered?
4. And in conclusion may I declare that I do not wish to accept the Greguss Medal in the present or in the future, neither alive nor dead.

89

Fortunately, it need not be assumed from this saga of persistent aggravation that Bartók's last years in Hungary were in any way stunted in achievement. In 1936, he gave his inaugural address to the Hungarian Academy of Sciences with a paper on 'Some Liszt Problems', a subject that had long fascinated him, and his performance of the solo part in Liszt's *Totentanz* for piano and orchestra, given as part of the composer's centenary celebrations, was talked about for many a year. Moreover, his opponents were justified in detecting an increase in official support for his music. In 1935, at long last, *The Wooden Prince* was seen again on the stage of the opera house to another overwhelming reception and a revival of *Duke Bluebeard's Castle* followed a year later. His more recent *Cantata Profana* was finally heard in Budapest a month later, albeit more than two years after its première by the BBC in London. Bartók felt sufficiently encouraged to enter again into the musical life of the city and, in 1938, the capital was finally able to hear the composer's own definitive performance of the *2nd Piano Concerto* under the baton of Ernest Ansermet.

In 1937 he began to assemble the *Mikrokosmos*, his unique collection of 153 instructive piano pieces, progressively graded from the elementary five finger exercises of Volume I to the demanding concert pieces of Volume VI. This compilation had occupied Bartók intermittently over a period of fourteen years, and it would be a short-sighted student who dismissed even the simplest ones as being beneath his attention, for their significance is far wider than their sterling pedagogic value. The collection is nothing less than a key to the world of its composer. Almost every facet of

In recital with Imre
Waldbauer.

Bartók's last concert in Vienna. Liszt's *Totentanz* with Dohnányi conducting.

his music is here, reduced to its barest essentials, and as such affords a priceless introduction to the world of modern music for the young pianist. Young Péter Bartók had a hand in the proving of this unusual masterpiece, as his father acknowledged.

In 1933, my little son Péter begged us to teach him to play the piano. I thought about it for a long time and finally, greatly daring, set to work on what was for me an unusual task. Apart from vocal and technical exercises the only music given to the child was taken from the *Mikrokosmos*; I hope this was good for him, but I must confess that I too learned a great deal from the experiment. . . .

By this time, Bartók was well into what is sometimes described as his 'classical' period. Certainly, he now composed with the orderly confidence and fluency of the great classical masters (witness the lightning speed with which he completed the *Fifth Quartet*) and although his formal procedures never ossified — he was always moulding and adapting his intricate structures — the experimentation with style and language was over. Virtually every bar

91

With his second son, Péter, the first young pianist to study *Mikrokosmos*.
(Embassy of the Hungarian People's Republic)

composed during the 1930s is immediately identifiable as quintessential Bartók; all influences are so deeply absorbed and synthesised as to have become integral parts of a single unified personality.

The three great works for Basle, the *Music for Strings, Percussion and Celesta*, the *Sonata for Two Pianos and Percussion* and the *Divertimento* have a unity of form and content that can truly be described as classical. Moreover, this fluency of inspiration which had taken wing in the *Fifth Quartet* did not desert him. The *Divertimento* and the *Sixth Quartet* (for his friend Zoltan Székely's New Hungarian Quartet) were almost entirely composed during a four week 'vacation' at Paul Sacher's chalet in Saanen. These commissions, as he reported with some satisfaction to his elder son Béla, 'make my situation similar to that of the old composers.'

If there were natural justice in this world, then this resolution and reconciliation of his artistic struggles would have presaged a peaceful and productive old age. That this was not to be can be laid at the door of the man who dashed the hopes and aspirations of so many at this time — Adolf Hitler.

As we have seen, the rise of Nazism had been a source of grave anxiety to Bartók from the beginning. Hungary was ripe for its doctrines, like a rotten apple ready to fall. The guiding principles of its leaders were expediency and opportunism. Bartók had been one of the first to complain about the exclusion of Jews from public positions and anti-semitism made further inroads during the premiership of General Gömbös who, while maintaining ostentatious friendships with Jewish industrialists, at the same time concluded a secret pact with Goering in 1935, which virtually undertook to turn Hungary into a Nazi-style state 'within two years.' After Gömbös' death in 1936, the rot continued and successive premiers vied with each other in ingratiating themselves with the mighty Third Reich, and were rewarded with the return of a disputed strip of Czechoslovakian territory which was held up to the people as a symbol of nationalistic independence. 'You can't imagine to what extent this has strengthened his (Hitler's) following in this country,' observed Bartók morosely.

Were it not for its evil cruelty, this sycophantic parade would sometimes appear to have elements of high farce, as in this anecdote from the career of Premier Béla Imredy, caustically related by Paul Ignotus:

In support of a Second Anti-Jewish Law which he published, with a picturesque touch of cruelty, on the eve of Christmas, 1938, he declared that 'one drop of Jewish blood' was enough to infect a man's character and patriotism. No sooner had he said so than he turned out to have more than one drop — a Jewish great-grandmother in his German-Bohemian ancestry. When the Regent (Horthy) at a dramatic audience showed him the relevant document, he fainted.

There was no humour in the situation for humanists like Bartók, nor for the thousands of Jews who headed for the free countries of Europe and America in order to escape the inevitable.

By this stage, open opposition would have been suicidal, so Bartók had to resort to subterfuge. He had refused to play in Italy or Germany for some time, but he had to invent a contractual pretext to prevent these countries from relaying a Hungarian Radio broadcast over their national networks.

Once again his thoughts turned to emigration, but the thought of having to take up teaching again, at the age of fifty-eight, to earn his living in a foreign country was so distressing that he 'could hardly bear to think about it.'

For the time being, he did not have to think about it, for he soon decided that it was out of the question to desert his aging and ailing mother in her last years. He expressed his mental and spiritual torment in a moving letter to Mrs Müller-Widman (now a regular

Brussels, 1938.

correspondent and confidante) in April, 1938, shortly after Hitler's take-over in Austria.

I think it is quite superfluous to write about this catastrophe — you have very concisely and eloquently put into words the main issue. This is exactly how we feel. There is one thing I want to add, concerning what is at this moment — at least for us — the most terrible prospect. That is the imminent danger that Hungary will surrender to this régime of thieves and murderers. The only question is — when and how? . . . So much for Hungary, where, unfortunately nearly all of our 'educated' Christians are adherents of the Nazi régime; I feel quite ashamed of coming from this class.

There were other practical problems to consider, too. After the *Anschluss*, Bartók had to urgently consider the question of his Austrian connections. Both he and Kodály were members of the Austrian branch of the Performing Rights Society and his publishers, Universal Edition, were also in Vienna. Within weeks, the German organisation STAGMA had taken over the PRS offices, and both Hungarians received a questionnaire to complete in order to establish their Aryan credentials to the satisfaction of the German authorities. Both refused angrily and Bartók used this 'illegal document' which, he claimed, infringed the statutes of the PRS, to transfer his membership to the London branch. He also concluded a hasty deal with the London firm of Boosey and Hawkes

Bartók with his eighty year old mother, whose age and frailty delayed his departure from Hungary.

who, opportunely, were looking to build up their list of contemporary music at the time and took over the publication of his works from then on.

Then there was the safety of his manuscripts to think about. He began to send them surreptitiously to his friends in Switzerland but, as the situation deteriorated still further, even this seemed a chancy way of ensuring their survival, so he wrote again to Mrs Müller-Widman:

I would like to ask you to send my manuscripts to my publishers, Boosey and Hawkes, 295 Regent Street, London . . . After all, London is further away from the land of the monsters.

Life was hectic. 'I have so much to do and arrange whenever I am in Budapest that it defies description,' he wrote, and yet he still had to find time for 'little money-making tours' abroad. With all the pressures that crowded in on him, it is hard to imagine how he found the time to compose. We must assume that he acted upon his own advice, given in response to a despondent letter from his American pupil Wilhelmine Creel:

As a musician, you should try to get through your difficulties by giving yourself entirely to your art.

Amidst this frenetic activity and growing apprehension two other works were born, remarkable instances of a great artist's ability to transcend and triumph over the adversities of external circumstances. The glowing, passionate *Violin Concerto*, written for his friend Zoltán Székely, established itself almost from birth alongside the concertos of Beethoven and Brahms as one of the very greatest of the genre. In lighter vein, *Contrasts* for violin, clarinet and piano, was commissioned by the great jazz clarinettist Benny Goodman (at the instigation of Szigeti) and fairly bubbles with swaggering *verbunkos* rhythms and bravura treatment of the two melody instruments (the piano has a surprisingly supportive rôle). The three artists recorded the work together for Columbia, in April, 1940, during Bartók's next visit to America.

Before this visit took place an event intervened which affected Bartók deeply and at the same time threw his plans into turmoil again. In December, 1939, Paula Bartók, who had struggled and suffered greatly to set her son on his path to greatness, died at the age of eighty-two. Bartók felt keenly his special debt to her, far beyond the ordinary bonds of filial devotion, and he suffered the inevitable pangs of remorse that he had perhaps neglected to attend to things which might have made her last years a little easier. At the same time he knew that the last tie which bound him to his homeland was now severed, and he set out for America with a heavy heart, but determined to pave the way for a new life.

When he returned to Budapest at the end of May, his official story for the press was that a further American tour had been arranged, starting in October, but his friends were in no doubt that his absence would be indefinite, perhaps permanent, and that the concert given by the Bartóks on October 8th was a farewell gesture. Ditta, who had recently been joining her husband on the platform in two-piano works, made her solo début in Mozart's Concerto in F. 'She played beautifully,' wrote Bartók, who had opened the evening with a performance of Bach's Concerto in A, and the couple united in a performance of Mozart's Concerto in E flat for Two Pianos under the direction of János Ferencsik.

The warmth of their reception from an audience which (according to a newspaper report) included 'the leading figures of our cultural life,' must have done much to ease the bitterness which, four days earlier, had prompted Bartók to add the following codicil to his will:

Recording *Contrasts* with Szigeti and Benny Goodman.

The farewell concert in
Budapest, October 8th, 1940.

. . . as long as there shall be any squares or streets in Hungary named after
these two men (Hitler and Mussolini) no square, street or public building
shall be named after me in this country; and until then no memorial plaque
shall be put in any public place.

Emotional farewells had to be curtailed to ensure that preparations for the voyage could be completed on time, and a few days
later the couple set out on their hazardous journey across war-torn
Europe to Lisbon, whence they sailed on October 20th.

Their feelings can easily be imagined, and they are poignantly
recorded in a letter to Mrs Müller-Widman from Geneva, the last
Bartók wrote from Europe.

It is hard, very hard to say farewell. And to see this wonderful country,
your country, perhaps for the last time, wondering all the time; what sort
of future awaits it and all our friends who are here!

Mrs Stefi Geyer came yesterday afternoon and was with us until this
evening, helping us and seeing us off. The voyage is, actually, like
plunging into the unknown from what is known but unbearable. If only on
account of my none too satisfactory state of health; I mean my peri-
arthritis, still incompletely cured. God only knows how and for how long
I'll be able to work over there. But we have no choice; it isn't at all a
question whether this has to happen; for it must happen.[1]

I send my thanks to you and your family for all the beauty, love and
friendship you have bestowed on me, and we send you every possible good
wish for the future.

1. In the original German text of this letter these words 'muss es sein; denn es muss sein'
   are a reference to the last movement of Beethoven's String Quartet, op. 135, where these
   words are inscribed over the two leading phrases.

Chapter Ten

Omens were not good as they stepped ashore in New York on October 30th. Most of their luggage had been held up for so long by the Spanish customs authorities that they had had to abandon it for fear of missing the connection to Lisbon. Their first concert was only four days hence, so they had to rush out and buy replacement evening clothes almost as soon as they arrived.

For the first few months, a reasonable income was assured from concert engagements, but this in itself made it all the more difficult to find time to attend to all the practical necessities. Early in December, they moved from their hotel into an apartment in Forest Hills, and in the meantime coped as best they could with the innumerable problems that beset them. Communications with Europe were slow and unreliable, but there were matters concerning his family at home that Bartók simply had to attend to, so endless hours were taken up with correspondence and enquiries about his Hungarian pension, his passport, currency, royalties, and, of course, the even more pressing business of the whereabouts of their luggage. In addition, they had to satisfy the US immigration regulations and they reported, in fairly good humour, to the local Post Office to have their finger-prints taken.

Bartók's last years in America were not happy ones, as is well known, and his feelings of disappointment and disillusion probably started from the beginning. Although he never expressed any sense of wounded pride, he must have felt hurt that his arrival in the USA was accorded so little attention. At this time, he well knew, European refugees were flooding into America in their millions, so it would have been unrealistic to expect that his sacrifice and personal stand against Nazism would arouse admiration or even recognition, but, whether he knew it or not, the previous wave of immigrant composers (such as Schoenberg, Stravinsky and Hindemith) had attracted far greater publicity. As it was, the couple felt bewildered and disorientated and were deeply grateful to the handful of friends, mostly Hungarian emigrés and former pupils like Wilhelmine Creel and Dorothy Parrish, who went out of their way to make them welcome.

A bright spot on the horizon was Bartók's research appointment

A two piano recital in New York Town Hall.

at Columbia University. In 1933, Milman Parry, then Harvard Professor of Classical Philology, had set out for Yugoslavia in pursuit of ethnic material which he hoped would yield connections with the Homeric epics. On his death in 1935, the material, which included over two thousand recordings of Serbo-Croatian folk songs, had been deposited with Columbia University. During his tour in the spring, Bartók had been invited to undertake the task of unravelling and classifying this collection under a temporary research fellowship funded by the Ditson Foundation. Even this arrangement was to be the source of disappointment and frustration as Bartók had not realised at the time that the appointment was not a secure one, but depended on funds being available for annual renewal. For the present, though, the prospect was an enticing one and, as a preliminary to his appointment, he was awarded an Honorary Doctorate by the university.

This sort of work was his natural habitat, but there were other aspects of American life to which he was less easily able to adapt, from the trivial,

human beings ruminating like cows (every second person is chewing gum); railway carriages in semi-darkness; the cheque-book system.

to the more serious matter of accommodation. They moved in May, 1941, to a quiet apartment in the Bronx, but up to then

we were piano-played and radio-blasted from right and left; a lot of noise came in from the street night and day; every five minutes we heard the rumble of the subway which made the very walls shake. Lastly, it took more than an hour to get to Columbia.

At least his work on the Parry collection took his mind off his worries for part of the day, but on every other front the clouds were gathering fast. His wife Ditta was not of the independent and resourceful mould of European immigrant, and her feelings of estrangement and depression were aggravated by her anxiety about their son Péter. It had always been the plan that he would rejoin the family as soon as he left school and his father had to expend valuable time and energy (not to mention lawyer's fees) in frustrating and protracted legal formalities to procure his entry visa. Bartók himself had to travel to Canada and re-enter the country to renew his own permit, which only gave him 'visitor's' status. But the most worrying thing was the financial insecurity which was becoming more threatening with each month that passed. Concert bookings for the coming season were not forthcoming and, for the first time, Bartók considered going home, on the grounds that,

if things are bad everywhere, one prefers to be at home.

Life would indeed have become unendurable were it not for the constant support of their friends. At this bleak moment in their lives the Bartóks were invited to spend the summer months in Vermont at the seaside home of Ágata Illés, whom they had met through their old friend Ernö Balogh, a former piano student in Budapest, who had emigrated after the first world war. Under the pseudonym Agatha Fassett, Miss Illés wrote a disconcertingly novelettish account of Bartók's last years under the title 'The Naked Face of Genius', but her kindness and concern was immeasurable. Wilhelmine Creel, too, did her utmost to secure a more advantageous academic post for Bartók at the University of Washington in Seattle, but he preferred to cling to his job at Columbia where he felt his involvement with Eastern European folk music preserved at least some links with his old life.

At the end of the summer, he was alarmed to discover that his arthritis was so bad that he could barely lift his arm to play the piano, and although it was greatly relieved by X-ray treatment, it was the prelude to more serious bouts of illness over the next eighteen months.

Their financial plight was becoming desperate, and in March, 1942, he wrote to Wilhelmine Creel,

All I can say is that never in my life since I earn my livelihood (that is from my twentieth year) have I been in such a dreadful situation as I will be probably very soon.

Everything about the current musical scene in America was against him. Royalties from European performances of his works could not be remitted to him because of the stringent currency restrictions in force everywhere, and performances of contemporary music in America were at their lowest ebb. The recording industry was virtually at a standstill owing to a dispute between the Musicians' Union and the recording companies, so there was no hope of work or publicity from that source.

In April, 1942, a single shaft of light penetrated the gloom when Péter Bartók was joyfully reunited with his parents after a hazardous journey lasting almost four months, and this probably confirmed their resolution to stay in America.

For over two years it had seemed that Bartók's creative spirit was broken, for he had composed not a note since his landing in America. He had just heard that his contract with Columbia University was unlikely to be renewed, although his work there was not half finished, but now, when his fortunes were at their lowest ebb, he took his first tentative steps towards a renewal of his powers. Another old and devoted friend, the conductor Frigyes (Fritz) Reiner, had arranged an appearance with the New York

With Fritz Reiner, a former pupil and one of Bartók's most dedicated champions in the U.S.A. (Corvina)

Philharmonic and for the occasion Bartók produced a *Concerto* for Two Pianos, Percussion and Orchestra, in fact a reworking of the Sonata. It is not one of his most successful achievements, as the addition of an orchestra merely dilutes and sometimes even nullifies the unique and delicately balanced *timbres* of the original, but it was perhaps the spark which rekindled his creative urge. Sadly, this concert was his last public appearance as a performer.

The disastrous financial implications of the termination of his contract with Columbia University were to some extent alleviated by an invitation from Harvard to give a series of lectures, starting in February 1943. His health was deteriorating steadily by now, and an evening temperature of over 100°F was a daily occurrence, while his weight had fallen to eighty-seven pounds. Doctors were baffled as to the cause of his condition and were therefore unable to propose treatment. As a result, he collapsed in the middle of a lecture at Harvard and was rushed to hospital. The horrified university authorities offered to pay all immediate expenses and, shortly afterwards, Ernö Balogh approached the American Society of Composers and Publishers who undertook to meet the cost of all further medical treatment.

Comprehensive tests at the hospital finally came up with the incontrovertible diagnosis of leukaemia, but Bartók was told that he had an obscure, but infinitely less alarming disease, polycithemia.

Meanwhile, his friends rallied around him in the most magnificent fashion. This was no easy task, for Bartók had a stubborn streak of resistance to anything which smacked of charity. Nevertheless, by the end of 1943 they had lifted the threat of financial disaster from his life and, from then on, his means, though modest, were never again a major source of anxiety.

Victor Bator, later to become the trustee of Bartók's Estate in

America and founder of the New York Bartók Archives, arranged for Columbia University to renew the research facility that meant so much to his friend, on the understanding that he and Szigeti would raise the additional funds required by subscription. Although the response from official bodies was poor, generous donations by private individuals, including Eugene Ormandy and Benny Goodman, ensured that this was done. Douglas Moore, chairman of the University Music Department, secured a donation from the relief fund of the National Institute of Arts and Letters which had to be deposited in Bartók's bank account in the guise of a prize award.

Finally, Serge Koussevitzky readily agreed to Szigeti's suggestion that he should commission an orchestral work with funds from the Koussevitzky Foundation which he had established in memory of his wife Natalie, a wealthy tea-heiress, and he visited Bartók in hospital to make the proposal personally. The suspicious composer at first refused to accept the thousand dollar cheque that the flamboyant conductor thrust in front of him then and there, protesting that he was in no position to undertake commitments that he might well be unable to fulfil for some time, if ever. Eventually a compromise was reached to pay half the fee immediately and the balance on completion.

Through the dedicated attention of his doctors, Bartók gained a temporary respite from the disease and at the end of June, through the continuing benevolence of ASCAP, he went to convalesce at Saranac Lake, NY. The creative spark which had flickered hesitantly at the beginning of the year now roared into flame and, when he returned to New York in October, he had with him the complete score of the *Concerto for Orchestra*. This was a tonic for everyone, and he could not have more amply repaid the loyalty and generosity of his friends and colleagues than with this life-enhancing symphony in five movements. The word 'concerto' is used in its baroque sense, and Bartók explained his choice of title 'by its tendency to treat the single instruments or instrument groups in a *concertante* or soloistic manner.' He described the grand design of the five movements as 'a gradual transition from the sternness of the first movement and the lugubrious death-song of the third, to the life-assertion of the last one.'

Koussevitzky was thrilled with the work and Bartók wrote with some relish to Wilhelmine Creel that he

said it is the best orchestra piece of the last 25 years (including the works of his idol Shostakovich!)

Bartók felt that Shostakovich's success had been out of all proportion to his worth as a composer, and in the fourth movement

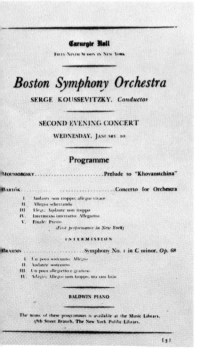

Programme for the premiere of
the *Concerto for Orchestra*,
Bartók's most popular
orchestral work.

of his *Concerto*, the 'Interrupted Serenade', a swooning Hungarian love song is obliterated by the raucous intrusion of the brass ('a band of rowdy drunkards', according to one interpretation) and there follows a snatch of trite fairground music which turns out to be a parody of Shostakovich's seventh symphony.

His doctors imposed strict limits on his activities, but they were persuaded to allow him to travel to Boston to attend the first performance in December 1944, by which time he was able to write,

For the next three years a modest living is assured for us.

There were still immense difficulties in collecting and transmitting royalties from Europe but Ralph Hawkes, the head of his English publishers, arranged to pay an annual advance of fourteen hundred dollars over and above anything that might be forthcoming from sales and royalties.

Another commission followed and in the most agreeable circumstances. Yehudi Menuhin, now safely through his *wunderkind* period and established in a great international career, had taken up the *Violin Concerto* and Bartók was entranced with his playing of this and also of the *1st Violin Sonata*.

He really is a great artist, (he wrote with enthusiasm) . . . It is altogether a happy thing that a young artist is interested in contemporary works which draw no public, and likes them and — performs them *comme il faut*.'

Menuhin's championship of the ailing composer did not stop short at 'liking and playing' his music, and soon after their first meeting, he commissioned a sonata for solo violin, and made many helpful suggestions of a practical nature in the course of its composition.

To avoid the rigours of a New York winter, Bartók retired, on doctors' advice, to the milder climate of Asheville, North Carolina. It was a beneficial move in every way.

At present I feel quite well, I have no temperature, my strength has returned, and I am able to take nice walks in the mountain forests — yes, I climb mountains (only very cautiously, of course). In March my weight was 87 lbs now it is 105 lbs.

and he not only completed the Sonata for Menuhin but also embarked on a massive scientific work on Romanian folk music, which eventually appeared in print in 1967, through the tireless endeavour of Benjamin Suchoff, Victor Bator's successor as Trustee of the New York Bartók Archives.

These were trying times for poor Ditta. She had no career as a pianist except as her husband's partner, and those days were now

103

One of the last photographs of Bartók. (Corvina)

over. The pain of her enforced separation from Béla was now compounded by Péter's enlistment in the US Navy. At the conclusion of a training course in electrical engineering, he was drafted to Panama for the rest of the war. They had given up their flat in Riverdale and moved into the Hotel Woodrow during Bartók's stay in hospital, and the outlook was still too uncertain to tackle the problem of finding a permanent home with any resolution. With the help and encouragement of friends, she was installed in a small two-room flat on the West Side and this became their last home in New York.

With the easing of their immediate worries concerning health and wealth, their thoughts turned increasingly to events in Europe and the fate of their country and loved ones at home, and they suffered agonies of suspense as a result of the garbled and conflicting reports that reached them.

In the latter part of 1944 they were able to re-establish some sort of orderly routine. They spent the summer at Saranac Lake again and the miraculous improvement in Bartók's health stabilised for a while. In February 1945 he contracted pneumonia, but even this responded quickly to the new wonder drug, penicillin.

They had been invited to spend the following summer with the Menuhins in Alma, California, but, at the last minute, Bartók felt unable to undertake the long journey and, besides, Ditta ('by way of variety') was not well herself at the time. So they headed once more for Saranac Lake, where the *3rd Piano Concerto* was all but completed, and work on a *Viola Concerto* for William Primrose reached an advanced stage.

On his demobilisation in August, Péter joined his parents at their summer retreat, but this happy reunion was almost immediately plunged into catastrophe. Bartók's condition deteriorated alarmingly and rapidly, and the family rushed back to New York early in September. For a week or two he was treated at home, where he continued to work on the piano concerto. On September 21st he was admitted to West Side Hospital and given blood transfusions, dextrose drips and oxygen, but these desperate measures only delayed the end for a few more days and he died on the 26th September.

The *3rd Piano Concerto*, his parting gift to his wife, Ditta, was complete but for the orchestration of the last seventeen bars, and his friend Tibor Serly was able to construct a plausible performing version of the *Viola Concerto* from the piano outline. Of a seventh string quartet, only jottings were on paper.

As his weary spirit and emaciated body sank beneath the weight of his illness, Bartók murmured to his doctor,

I am only sorry to be going with my luggage full.

Chapter Eleven

Bartók was a solitary man, a 'loner'. At an early stage in his career, he developed a stubborn integrity which won him more admiration than affection, except from a small handful of really close friends. From the early 1920s he had absolute conviction in his stature as a composer, and he clearly felt that his time would come. The Hungarian scholar, Bence Szabolcsi, compared Bartók's relationship with his public to that of Beethoven. Like Beethoven's, his new works were often met with angry incomprehension and then, as they became accepted, his latest productions were condemned as wilful novelties and compared disparagingly with the earlier ones. It was particularly hard, then, that his American works, the *Concerto for Orchestra* and the *3rd Piano Concerto*, should suffer the sneers of certain critics and musicians, this time on account of their alleged 'commercialism'. Bartók had gone soft, they said, and was pandering to the American masses, though the gritty *Sonata for Solo Violin* should have been enough to disabuse them of this notion. In fact, the simplicity, directness and radiance of these works continue a trend that had begun to manifest itself in works he composed before he left Hungary, notably the *Violin Concerto* and the *Divertimento*. To decry it as cheap populism was sheer intellectual snobbery. If we stand back and look at Bartók's output as a whole, we can see it as a great arch from the naïve romantic excess of *Kossuth* to the unforced and humane intelligibility of the *3rd Piano Concerto*, an arch which reaches its apex in the extreme harshness and dissonance of the works written in his forties in the period roughly spanned by *The Miraculous Mandarin* and the *Fourth String Quartet*. Viewed in this way, the increasing clarity and lucidity of his 'classic' period — the 1930s — leads naturally and inevitably to this last American phase.

Since his death, Bartók research has become a thriving industry for musicologists, especially in Hungary. Scarcely a year passes which does not yield some new revelation to their persistent probing. A Béla Bartók Archive has been set up as a permanent department of the Hungarian Academy of Sciences and in 1981, the centenary of the composer's birth, a Bartók Museum was opened in the house of Csalan Street, Budapest, where the family lived from

1932 to 1940. The music has been analysed, it would seem, from every conceivable angle and the results have sometimes proved startling. Ernö Lendvai, in his brilliant study *Béla Bartók; An Analysis of his Music* (1971) caught the academic world napping when he disclosed that several of Bartók's works conformed very precisely to Golden Section proportion, a phenomenon observed in ancient Greek and Egyptian architecture. No one has been able to deny this demonstrably mathematical fact, but there are still eminent scholars who claim that it was fortuitous, not deliberate.

Tonal axes, Fibinaccian series, heptatonic scales, polymetric synchronisation and all the other paraphernalia of Bartók analysis lie well beyond the scope of this general biography, but the interested reader is directed to Laszlo Somfai's admirable résumé of these findings in the Bartók entry in *The New Grove's Dictionary of Music and Musicians*.

The first serious analysis of Bartók's music was undertaken in 1930 by a German musicologist Edwin von der Nüll, and it is always wise to bear in mind Bartók's comments on that occasion:

. . . in spite of all honest efforts, with such things intuition plays a far more prominent rôle than one would imagine. All of my music and, last but not least, this problem of harmonisation depend on instinct and emotion. It is no good asking why I wrote a passage as I did, instead of putting it differently — I can only reply that I wrote down what I felt. Let the music speak for itself; it surely speaks clearly enough to assert itself.

Bartók's international reputation was not really established until the late 1920s, so was not a factor in the movements which, in the two preceding decades, determined the course of European twentieth century music. Hence, he founded and left no 'school' and pursued his musical career with the same solitary idealism as he led his private life. And yet Bartók, perhaps most of all the great twentieth century composers, has reached the hearts of concert audiences in the way that apologists have always predicted for their avant-garde heroes, while other notable, even great figures are still more cherished by scholars and musicians than by the public at large. It may seem odd that Bartók, whose uncompromising intellectual discipline would seem likely to discourage the uninitiated and whose preoccupation with localised folk song would seem to make him exclusive, if not parochial in appeal, should win this genuine popularity whilst others have retained an intimidating relationship with concert goers. Yet this is surely a measure of the greatness of the man; that, of all the accepted masters of the first half of this century, he speaks with the most universal appeal. Like Bach and Beethoven before him, he possessed that rarest of gifts, to express the most complex thoughts and feelings with a directness that explains itself to the receptive ear.

It is sad that in his life he rarely experienced the same warmth of communication that his music has enjoyed posthumously. And yet his work was by far the greater part of his life, and in that he no doubt achieved a certain rarefied happiness that is not attainable to lesser men. Towards the end, he looked wistfully again towards Hungary, 'I should like to return home, and that for good,' and the Provisional Hungarian National Government, set up by the Russians at the end of 1944, elected him a member *in absentia*.

Modern Hungarian biographers tend to blame his difficulties onto the reactionary forces that controlled Hungary between the wars. But Bartók had been just as scathing in his condemnation of the short-lived communist Republic of Councils of 1919:

Protectionism and bureaucracy flourished as never before. The Councils' Government was just as narrow-minded as the former bourgeois administrations had been.

So it is doubtful whether, granted good health, he could have settled happily into an official position in the Soviet-dominated post-war establishment. He had long since decided to go his own way, to do nothing with which he could reproach himself and to shut his face to compromise and the fickleness of official approval. Ernst Roth, an executive of the publishers, Boosey and Hawkes, perhaps enshrined his life more pithily than anyone when he wrote,

It was his misfortune to have been born and to live in such troubled times; for ultimately they overwhelmed him.

Selected Bibliography

Ferenc Bónis: Béla Bartók—*His Life in Pictures and Documents*.
Boosey and Hawkes, London, 1972

ed. János Deményi: *Béla Bartók Letters*.
Faber & Faber, London, 1971

Agatha Fassett: *The Naked Face of Genius—Béla Bartók's Last Years*.
Gollancz, London, 1958

Paul Ignotus: *Hungary*. Ernest Benn Ltd., London, 1972

Lajos Lesznai: *Béla Bartók*. J. M. Dent & Sons, London, 1973

Serge Moreux: *Béla Bartók*. Harvill Press, London, 1953

Halsey Stevens: *The Life and Music of Béla Bartók*.
New York University Press, 1953/1964

ed. Benjamin Suchoff: *Béla Bartók Essays*.
Faber & Faber, London, 1976

József Ujfalussy: *Béla Bartók*. Corvina Press, Budapest, 1971

Percy M. Young: *Zoltán Kodály*. Ernest Benn Ltd., London, 1964

List of Works

Note: Juvenile works (i.e. works composed before 1900) are not listed. Several works by Bartók exist in more than one version (i.e. orchestrations, transcriptions, etc.). Only the original versions are given here. For a complete list of Bartók's works, see Grove's Dictionary of Music and Musicians.

Stage Works

1911	Duke Bluebeard's Castle, opera in one act	46, 51, 52, 84, 90
1917	The Wooden Prince, ballet in one act	51, 53, 59, 87, 90
1919	The Miraculous Mandarin, pantomime in one act	51, 59, 60, 73, 82, 105

Orchestral Works (including Concertos)

1901	Rhapsody no. 1 for piano and orchestra	25, 26
1903	'Kossuth' — Symphonic Poem for full orchestra	22, 24, 25, 105
1904	Scherzo for piano and orchestra	25, 40
1905	Suite no. 1 for orchestra	30
1905-7	Suite no. 2 for orchestra	39
1908	Violin Concerto no. 1	26
1907-16	Two Portraits for orchestra	41
1910	Two Pictures for orchestra	41, 42
1912	Four Pieces for orchestra	
1923	Dance Suite for orchestra	63, 66, 68
1926	Piano Concerto no. 1	69, 70
1928	Rhapsody no. 1 for violin and orchestra	74, 76
1928	Rhapsody no. 2 for violin and orchestra	74, 76
1931	Piano Concerto no. 2	84
1938	Violin Concerto no. 2	90, 95, 101, 105
1939	Divertimento for string orchestra	78, 92, 105
1943	Concerto for orchestra	102, 105
1945	Piano Concerto no. 3	104, 105
1945	Viola Concerto (reconstructed and orchestrated by Tibor Serly)	104

Chamber Music

1903	Sonata for violin and piano	22
1904	Piano Quintet	22, 25, 26
1908	String Quartet no. 1	42
1917	String Quartet no. 2	51
1921	Sonata for violin and piano, no. 1	22, 26, 68
1922	Sonata for violin and piano, no. 2	68
1927	String Quartet no. 3	73
1928	String Quartet no. 4	73, 105
1931	44 Duos for two violins	
1934	String Quartet no. 5	84, 91, 92
1937	Sonata for two pianos and percussion	78, 92
1938	'Contrasts' for violin, clarinet and piano	95
1939	String Quartet no. 6	92
1940	Sonata for solo violin	105

Piano Music

1900	Variations on a theme by F.F.
1903	4 Pieces 22
1907	3 Hungarian Folk Songs
1908	14 Bagatelles 39, 41
1908	10 Easy Pieces
1909	2 Elegies 41
1908-9	For Children (43 pieces in 4 volumes) 39
1910	2 Romanian Dances 41
1908-10	7 Sketches 42
1910	4 Dirges 42
1908-11	3 Burlesques 42
1911	Allegro Barbaro 44, 69
1915	Sonatina 48, 75
1915	6 Romanian Folk Dances 48, 49
1915	20 Romanian Christmas Songs
1916	Suite 50
1914-18	15 Hungarian Peasant Songs
1918	3 Studies 62
1920	8 Improvisations on Hungarian Peasant Songs 61, 69
1926	Sonata 69
1926	'Out of Doors' 69, 70
1926	9 Little Piano Pieces 69
1916-27	3 Rondos
1926-39	Mikrokosmos (153 pieces in 6 volumes) 90, 91

Vocal Music (all for voice and piano)

1904	4 Hungarian Folk Songs
1905	'To the Little "Tót",' (5 songs)
1906	20 Hungarian Folk Songs (in collaboration with Kodály) 31
1907	4 Slovakian Folk Songs
1915-16	5 Songs (texts compiled by K. Gombossy) 51
1916	5 Songs (texts by E. Ady) 27, 51
1907-17	8 Hungarian Folk Songs
1924	Village Scenes 66
1929	20 Hungarian Folk Songs (in 4 volumes) 84
1945	Ukrainian Folk Song

Choral Music

1910	4 Old Hungarian Folk Songs, for 4 part male chorus, a cappella
1915	2 Romanian Folk Songs, for 4 part female chorus, a cappella
1917	5 Slovak Folk Songs, for 4 part male chorus, a cappella
1917	4 Slovak Folk Songs, for 4 part mixed chorus and piano
1930	4 Hungarian Folk Songs, for mixed chorus, a cappella 84
1930	'Cantata Profana', for tenor and baritone soloists, double mixed chorus and orchestra 83, 90
1932	6 Székely Songs, for 6 part male chorus, a cappella 84
1935	25 Choruses for 2 and 3 part children's choir, with and without accompaniment
1935	'From Olden Times', for 3 part male chorus, a cappella

Index

Illustrations in bold type